"Anchored on the bedrock of Jain tradition, Aidan Rankin provides us with compelling ideas to address the environmental crisis of our time."

Ian Mowll, Coordinator, GreenSpirit Network, UK

"Aidan Rankin offers an innovative and exciting perspective on ethical practices for daily life, business and our relationship with the environment through the ancient tradition of Jainism. He provides practical wisdom and guidance on how we can draw upon Jain ideas in rebalancing our economic and social priorities."

Lynne Sedgmore CBE, PhD, Former CEO, Centre for Excellence in Leadership and 157 Group, UK

"Jainism's message, as this succinct book brings out so well, is that all forms of life are in some way connected. Dr Rankin tells the story of what Jainism is and what it means to be a Jain."

Werner Menski, Emeritus Professor of South Asian Law, SOAS, University of London, UK

Jainism and Environmental Philosophy

Environmental policy agendas, activism and academic research into ecological questions are all predominantly derived from the philosophical perspectives of the West. At national and global levels, environmental policy-makers tend to work according to Western-based methodologies. At the same time, emergent or developing economies are profoundly affected by the issues they address, including air pollution, rapid urban expansion, habitat loss and climate change.

If environmental awareness, and the policies that stem from it, are to have a lasting global impact, it is important that non-Western voices are heard in their own right, and not merely as adjuncts of Western-led agendas. Jain thought is a useful case study of a system of values in which environmental protection and the idea of a 'web of life' are central, but which has evolved in India independently of Western environmentalism. This book describes and explains Jain environmental philosophy, placing it in its cultural and historical context while comparing and contrasting with more familiar or 'mainstream' forms of ecological thought. It will also show how this thought translates into practice, with an emphasis on the role of environmental concerns within the business and commercial practices of Jain communities. Finally, the book examines the extent to which Jain ideas about environmental protection and interconnectedness have universal relevance.

This book will be of great interest to students and scholars of environmental ethics, sustainable business and economics, environmental policy, and Jainism.

Aidan Rankin is an author, independent scholar and property consultant based in London, UK.

Routledge Focus on Environment and Sustainability

The Application of Science in Environmental Impact Assessment
Aaron Mackinnon, Peter Duinker and Tony Walker

Jainism and Environmental Philosophy
Karma and the Web of Life
Aidan Rankin

Jainism and Environmental Philosophy

Karma and the Web of Life

Aidan Rankin

LONDON AND NEW YORK

from Routledge

First published 2018
by Routledge
2 Park Square, Milton Park, Abingdon, Oxon OX14 4RN

and by Routledge
711 Third Avenue, New York, NY 10017

Routledge is an imprint of the Taylor & Francis Group, an informa business

© 2018 Aidan Rankin

British Library Cataloguing-in-Publication Data
A catalogue record for this book is available from the British Library

Library of Congress Cataloging-in-Publication Data
A catalog record for this book has been requested

ISBN: 978-1-138-55182-4 (hbk)
ISBN: 978-1-315-14778-9 (ebk)

Typeset in Times New Roman
by Out of House Publishing

For Brian

Contents

Foreword

While it is undeniable that Jainism is an ancient minority religion, and has always been in that non-hegemonic position, it is remarkable how clear-sighted and deeply rational this early philosophical tradition has been from the very beginning. It is even more remarkable how relevant the core teachings of this particular minoritarian approach to understanding the world remain for today's troubled, chaotic times. Notably, this tradition does not even believe in or employ any God as a global CEO who manages everything on some kind of divine supercomputer, keeping accounts of everyone's good and bad deeds. And yet, this does not leave the individual Jain on a desert island, stranded, without guidance and advice. It teaches, basically, that everyone is his or her own guru, and that self-controlled ordering, to the best of one's abilities and potential, is the key to progress. This is at once a deeply onerous, but also an amazingly empowering core message, built on the basic principle or *Grundnorm*, as I would call it, of everything being connected.

Jainism's message, as this succinct book brings out so very well, I found, attempts a rephrasing, suitable for and conditioned by our time and age, of the ancient realisation that all forms of life are in some way connected. It seeks to tell the story of what Jainism is and what it means to be a Jain. This indicates that all the different life forms, as tiny as they may be, including the most noxious germs and also plankton, need to be accounted for and somehow managed by human actors in ways that are idealistically based on harmonious forms of interaction. One major form of such interaction may then simply be avoidance of contact, abstaining from getting close to dangerous elements and/or refraining from becoming involved with all kinds of ethically and morally questionable entities, practices and even thoughts. These modes of various verbal but evidently mainly non-verbal interactions, and often completely invisible forms of communication, should all be conducted basically as non-violently as possible. The aim is that all stakeholders in this global spider web of cosmic interrelatedness are allowed to live on and make their contributions to the never-ending cycle of existence. Realising this grand scheme, and one's own minuscule and yet engaged and active place in it, says this book rather convincingly, represents an alternative form of Enlightenment.

The main purpose of this book is to explain in an accessible manner how being a Jain, Jain *Dharma* or Jainness, works out in practice as well as in theory. The book also asks and discusses how this can contribute to wider worldviews of the environment. The overarching themes of non-violence and its collateral aim of reduction of harm are deeply and curiously in tune with ecological concerns that also nourish notions of sustainable enterprise. Dr Rankin's book distinguishes Jain approaches to such ecologically based thinking from that of environmentalists who often seem to eschew profit and economics, because they construct or perceive an inherent contradiction between environment and development. This book explains very well, I think, that this binary thinking of either/or is itself deeply problematic. It is just not connected to the pluralities of lived reality. Instead, the many-sidedness of perspectives, a remarkably postmodern form of vision, is preferred and advised. The doctrine of multiple viewpoints is presented as an endless quest, akin to striving for the ideals of justice and 'rule of law', in the celebration and recognition of diversity and difference. Here it becomes clear again that Jainism comes from a minority perspective, constantly reminding all participants in communication that 'we are all in this together'.

In the commercial sphere, Jain-run business is placed in an interdependent relationship of connectedness and hence there is also no separation between environment and commercial activity. The book's conclusion is entirely convincing, namely that this is an eminently practical and pragmatic system of thought. Jainism (or more accurately Jain *Dharma* as the author explains) appears as a form of culture-specific natural law, which has at the same time universal features as well as maintaining a focus on individual salvation. It is a form of 'religion' and a tradition that can and needs to be lived, not timetabled into some special slots. It is also a wonderful example of a tradition that can be understood and appreciated by outsiders without having formally to 'convert' to that tradition.

Werner Menski
Emeritus Professor of South Asian Law
SOAS, University of London

Acknowledgements

I would like to thank Jacqueline Curthoys, of Routledge, Commissioning Editor for my previous book *Jainism and Ethical Finance*, for inspiring me to write about Jain environmental thought. My two Commissioning Editors, Annabelle Harris and Hannah Ferguson, provided friendly support and encouragement during this project. It has been a stroke of extreme good fortune to work with Matthew Shobbrook as Editorial Assistant. I am also grateful to Mark Wells for his excellent and indispensable work as indexer. Lynne Sedgmore CBE has been another source of support, friendship and encouragement, as has Professor Werner Menski, who has generously contributed the Foreword. Many Jains have contributed to this project. Professor Kanti Mardia, in particular, has taught me to look for hidden connections between ancient spiritual insights and modern scientific discoveries. Brian Scoltock has put up with me patiently throughout the writing of this book: his belief in the project has been crucial to me at all times. My mother, Anne Vannan Rankin, first taught me the principle of *Ahimsa*, or compassion for all forms of life, and my father, Professor David Rankin, has been a constant source of wise advice.

With the Jain motto, *Parasparopagraho Jivanam* (All life is bound together), I express thanks to all those who have contributed, directly or indirectly, to the completion of this book.

1 Introduction

> Jains do not believe in any external God who created and sustains the world, neither do they believe in any means of redemption outside themselves. The individual ... must ultimately find the truth for himself as no priest or scripture is believed to have all the answers. [Jain] principles are intended to be self-verifying so that the follower discovers truths for himself rather like a research worker in a laboratory.
>
> K.V. Mardia, *The Scientific Foundations of Jainism* (2007: pp. 4–5)

The jewel of Right Conduct

As a non-theistic belief system, Jainism is primarily concerned with the way in which individuals find their way towards personal enlightenment. It is a transcendent faith tradition, in that its view of the enlightened individual is ultimately as a liberated being cut loose from the world. Yet it is at the same time a highly practical philosophy that, as Jain mathematician Kanti Mardia says, lends itself to scientific endeavour (Mardia, *op. cit.*, pp. 4–5) and enables individuals and communities to re-evaluate their relationship with their surroundings. This practical emphasis has helped to establish Jains in the professions, business and skilled crafts where, as the example of the jewellery trade illustrates, commercial success is underscored by a strong ethical code.

When Jyoti Kothari, owner of Vardhaman Gems in the Indian city of Jaipur, Rajasthan, described the principles by which jewellers from the Jain cultural tradition have operated through the centuries, he emphasised that the gemstone and jewellery trade is regarded as *alparambhi*, or 'requiring minimum violence' (Kothari 2004: pp. 48–50). In their native India and their scattered global communities, Jains have been successful jewellers. Jains of Gujarati and Rajasthani heritage play a powerful if low-key role in the jewellery sector of Antwerp, one of the prime global centres for the trade in polished diamond (Hofmeester 2013; Lum 2014; Meena Peters 2014; Shah and Rankin 2017). The jewellery industry is an attractive option for a culture that seeks to avoid inflicting harm or *himsa* on the living Earth. In this context, the industry is defined as the jewellers craft of creating fine objects out of gems and precious metals, the skills associated with gem identification and grading along with the trade in jewellery and gemstones. It does not refer to the process of gemstone extraction, which is unlikely to be undertaken by devout Jains as it involves direct physical interference with nature and possible danger to living organisms. The peaceful production of beautiful objects and the jeweller or gemstone grader's lack of violence against people or ecosystems has made these occupations, in Kothari's words, 'ideal for Jains wishing to adhere to the principle of Ahimsa' (Kothari 2004: pp. 48–50).

To Jains themselves, and more especially to external observers, the outstanding characteristic of their philosophy as enacted in everyday life is its emphasis on non-violence: 'The most important principle of Jainism is that of non-violence in thought and deed towards not only fellow humans, but even the smallest forms of life' (2007: p. 4). Non-violence is an incomplete translation of the word *Ahimsa*, which more literally means 'non-injury' or the avoidance of harm. It is the first vow (*vrata*) undertaken by ascetics and in a more moderate form by lay people, and it is lived out in more a literal way by the ascetics (male and female) who often go to extreme lengths to avoid injuring even the smallest forms of life.

Ahimsa means more than adopting a pacific stance and a vegetarian diet, although the latter plays an important role in Jain popular culture. As a philosophy of life, it requires a recalibration of the relationship between humanity and 'the rest' of nature, so that human creativity is no longer seen as a justification or excuse for the domination of other species or manipulation of the environment. Instead, our relationship with nature is approached from a position of humility. Assumptions of a human right to dominance by virtue of supposedly superior intelligence yield necessarily to the belief in a human responsibility to conserve and protect. This is part of a larger sense that humankind is embedded in nature rather than in some way outside or above it. Hence all life, including human life, is mutually dependent. All living organisms play an important and distinctive part in the functioning of the Earth (and the 'inhabited universe'). The smaller the unit of life, the more powerful and subtle its function is likely to be. This position, arrived at through meditation and lived experience, is now increasingly echoed by the physical sciences. Oceanographers, for instance, conduct detailed studies of the role of plankton in regulating the temperature of the sea and thus influencing global climate (Fortey 1998: pp.122–157). A species once dismissed as basic and unimportant is now widely recognised as essential to the equilibrium of the planet. In Jain communities, such conclusions have been more or less taken for granted for at least two millennia. To them, a respectful and interdependent relationship with the natural world is not only 'right' from an ethical standpoint, but also a form of rational self-interest.

In the context of the Jaipur jewellery trade, Kothari explains that it is still based on human scale craftsmanship in small workshops where environmental impact is kept to the minimum. Skills are transmitted between generations of extended families, with employers and workers often related to each other. As part of his wider training, the apprentice is instructed in the traditional ethos and values of the industry. The skills of the jeweller, such as gemstone identification, grading and valuation, are transmitted from master to pupil in a relationship resembling that of guru and disciple:

> The teacher nurture(s) his students with the qualities required of a true jeweller, whilst equipping them with the necessary practical skills and theoretical knowledge of the trade. They [are] taught to be patient, calm, vigilant, creative and diplomatic, fitting the sort of values Jains were traditionally taught. Jain jewellers [have] functioned according to the following basic rules in particular: imitations were never to be sold as real; substituting of goods was treated as a major offence; a certain percentage was deducted in every transaction for charitable purposes.
>
> (Kothari 2004: pp. 48–50)

The ethos absorbed by the student is part of his practical training and not, as is so often the case with Western educational techniques, an add-on or a separate 'academic component'. Values are treated as essential to the performance of the jeweller's craft, which requires careful action from its practitioners. The concept of Careful Action (*irya-samiti*) in Jainism will be one of the central themes of this book. Irya-samiti, which more literally means 'care in walking' or 'careful movement', is one of five *samiti* (rules of conduct) undertaken by ascetics. By moving carefully, harm to small life forms is reduced to a minimum. Careful Action (as we shall refer to it below) influences lay Jains as well, playing a critical role in the way they approach the environment in general and, in particular, seek to operate their businesses along sustainable lines. In the jeweller's profession, it involves avoiding the greed or lust for possessions (*Parigraha*) that can easily accompany contact with gemstones, but valuing their intricacy and natural beauty instead. Honesty, respect for the customer and consideration for the environment are among the most important parts of the traditional jeweller's training.

Furthermore, the link between jewellery and spiritual practice is made explicit in major philosophical and religious treatises such as the *Kalpasutra* (first century CE), in which gem identification is listed as one of 72 principal skills to be acquired by men. In the fourteenth century CE, a court jeweller in Delhi named Thakur Theru published the *Ratnapariksha* (*Gem Inspection Manual*), a text in which commercial and spiritual instruction are intertwined. There is also the story of Trishala, mother of Vardhamana Mahavira, the *Tirthankara* ('ford-maker' or enlightened teacher) most revered by Jains today and after whom Vardhaman Gems is named. In the penultimate of fourteen auspicious dreams before her son's birth, Trishala saw heaps of jewels appearing before her. The image of the jewel is applied to the concept of *Anekantavada* (many-sidedness), a highly distinctive area of Jain thought that strongly influences attitudes towards the environment (see Chapter 4). Each *naya* (viewpoint) is likened to one of the facets of a cut diamond, so that the same clear light can be perceived from many angles. Jains are also enjoined to live according to the Three Jewels or 'Triple Gems' (*Ratnatraya* or *Triratna*): *Samyak Darshana* (Right Vision), *Samyak Gyana* (or *Jnana*) (Right Knowledge) and *Samyak Charitra* (Right Conduct).

The way of life of the Jain jewellers of Rajasthan, and the philosophy that underpins it, exemplify many of the notable characteristics of Jain communities, including apparent contradictions and paradoxes. Highly traditionalist at one level, companies like Vardhaman Gems are simultaneously open to the world and an important part of the outward looking India of the twenty-first century. They make full use of the Internet and keep abreast of the latest technological developments, drawing upon a rich tradition of internationalism, immigration and trade across borders (see Chapter 5) while preserving strong local and communal roots. Like other Jain businesses, they combine Careful Action – the principle of living lightly and minimising environmental impact – with the maximising of profit.

For Western environmental activists especially, this link between commercial success and the minimising of harm to nature can seem confusing or problematic. The green movement as it has emerged since the late twentieth century has tended to include a critique of capitalism

(Porritt 1984; Dobson 2007; Klein 2008; Klein 2015). More difficult still from the perspective of ecological thought is the cultural emphasis on accumulating wealth combined with the rejection of Parigraha or material desire. Jain communities are primarily business-centred and the focus of these businesses is, not surprisingly, profit and material success. This would appear to conflict with the powerful strand in eco-philosophy that rejects materialism and wealth accumulation as inherently dangerous to the environment, favouring a 'simpler way' or 'living as if nature mattered' and eschewing materialism and production for profit (Trainer 1985; Devall and Sessions 1985; Devall 1990). The social and economic status of most Jains contradicts such aspirations to 'return to nature'. Only the ascetics, a tiny minority of the Jain population, renounce material goods, but for them the practice of austerities and transcendence of the material world matter more than living in harmony with nature (Jaini 2001). Finally, Jain businesses tend to be family concerns (Shah and Rankin 2017: pp. 89–92) from which non-family members and non-Jains are excluded. This position conflicts with the commitment to equality and diversity that is usually so central to environmentalist campaigning and green political programmes in the Western world.

Such contradictions are real and so it is tempting to conclude that Jain philosophy has only a partial relevance to environmental philosophy in the twenty-first century, including its strong sub-themes of political pluralism and living in an interconnected world (Dundas 2004). Yet Jains have been widely acknowledged as pioneers of environmental thought (Marshall 1995). Their belief in refraining from harm to the natural world and their sense that all living systems are interconnected can be instantly recognised by environmental thinkers and campaigners alike. That sense of connectedness, of being part of a 'web of life', calls to mind the cosmology and worldview of 'indigenous' societies such as Native Americans (Peat 2006). Jainism is an indigenous philosophy in the sense that it traces its origins to the earliest Indian thought, before the emergence of what is now known as Hinduism. However it is also a philosophy highly attuned to the modern world, with a scientific and rationalist approach to balance its powerful intuitive currents. Again problematically for many environmentalists, the web of life is not a neutral or wholly beneficent force, but a karmic encasement from which the ultimate goal is escape (see Chapter 3). These differences arise because Jainism offers a non-Western approach to environmental philosophy, rooted in the varied cultures and historical experiences of the Indian subcontinent and its peoples. When this philosophy is viewed on its own terms, rather than through the prevailing ideological prisms of green thought, the apparent paradoxes often turn out to be creative tensions or points on a continuum.

Jains derive their thinking from an extensive corpus of philosophical and spiritual writings. Theirs has always been a minority tradition, a flame carefully kept alive by small and scattered communities that can seem to the outsider to be introspective or at times unwelcoming. Its riches, spiritual as much as material, are largely hidden from view. The purpose of this book is two-fold. First, it aims to offer a glimpse into the way Jains think and carry their thoughts into practice. Secondly, it addresses the question of how – or even whether – the Jain worldview can contribute to the wider global development of environmental philosophy and its practical expressions.

The distinctiveness of Jainism

At a global level, the Jains are a community of between 5 and 10 million people, concentrated in India but with Diaspora populations in eastern and southern Africa, North America, Europe and Australia. In India, the Jain community numbers just below 5 million and is noted for its high literacy rate, 94.1 per cent compared with a national average of 65.38 per cent. Significantly, they have the nation's highest female literacy rate, 90.1 per cent in comparison with the national average of 54.16 per cent (Chakrawertti 2004). These statistics, drawn from the Indian national census of 2001, owe much to the Jains' high regard for education and the pursuit of knowledge. Education, in this context, includes the forms of highly skilled apprenticeship portrayed by Jyoti Kothari above. It is by no means limited to exclusively academic study and encompasses lived experience, philosophical inquiry and the exercise of critical reason.

Ultimately, each individual is regarded as his or her own guru, and yet despite the existence of different forms or schools of Jain thought there is a surprising absence of sectarian conflict. This lack of factionalism arises in large part from one of the distinctive features of Jain culture. Its adherents share a belief in the exercise of tolerance. They view dogmatic or inflexible ideologies as a manifestation of *Ekant* (or *Ekantika*), a form of 'one-sidedness' or doctrinaire certainty that is an obstacle both to spiritual progress and objective truth. In Jain thought, there is no distinction between the quest for scientific knowledge, including greater understanding of the universe, and the quest for spiritual enlightenment. Both processes undermine and eventually break the cycle of *Avidya*, the ignorance or lack of perception that holds humanity back. It is Avidya, for example, that leads to a distorted relationship between humankind and the environment, arising as it does from lack of scientific understanding of nature and spiritual affinity with it.

India's Jains are one of the most successful business communities in the country and by some measures have the nation's highest per capita income (Chakrawertti 2004). Overwhelmingly a population of city-dwellers, they are a powerful presence in professions such as medicine and law. This pattern is repeated in the Diaspora, where the Jain story is one of high educational attainment followed by achievement in business, finance and the professions. Diaspora Jains have for the most part achieved a judicious blend of integration with their host communities and preserving, often with extreme care, their underlying cultural values.

The word 'Jainism' is used for convenience at many points in this book because it is the term generally understood outside the Jain community. Many Jains nonetheless have ambivalent feelings about the word and some reject it altogether. This is because they consider the concept of an '-ism', with its implication of a narrowly defined ideological agenda, as an insufficient or misleading way to present their doctrines and way of life. Jain theories and practices are components of *Dharma*, which is simultaneously a cosmology, an ethical system with the ultimate goal of spiritual liberation or *Moksha*, and a practical code for everyday living. The phrase 'Jain Dharma' is therefore used below as often as possible as a replacement for '-ism'. An approximate translation of the Sanskrit word Dharma is 'cosmic order' and this concept transcends the prevalent Western understanding of 'philosophy', 'religion', 'faith' or 'ethos'. All these terms will also be used at times where they seem most relevant or descriptive. From the standpoint of practising Jains, they are intersecting parts of a larger 'whole'. In the same way, sitting meditation, reverence for the Tirthankaras, charitable giving – including support for the *Panjrapoor* (animal hospitals or sanctuaries) – and the conscious avoidance of harm to other species are all aspects of Dharmic practice that reinforce each other.

Jain Dharma is also more than a series of doctrines lived out with varying degrees of success by loyal adherents. It is a cultural and aesthetic sensibility, reflected in the serene images of the Tirthankaras in painting and sculpture, the detached, omniscient 'peaceful warriors' (Pal 1994) liberated from all earthly concerns, including dependence on the rest of nature. At the heart of this disposition is a sense of perspective on the individual, society and the world based on long-term thinking and an understanding of the universe as vast, eternal and cyclical. Mardia refers to the sensibility shared by many Jains as 'Jain-ness', an idea that combines the intuitive and eco-centric components of the Dharma with its rationalist, humanistic and transcendent aspects:

> Jainness is concerned with reconciling continuity and change, possibility and limitation. It offers the possibility for spiritual liberation through self-knowledge, while accepting the mental and physical limits of the human form. ... Rather than seeing to impose its own truths, [Jain Dharma] asks us to look inside ourselves, find our own truth and continually question it.
>
> (Mardia and Rankin 2013: p. 26)

The central role of the individual distinguishes Jain doctrines from those of most schools of Hinduism and Buddhism, which emphasise the ultimate transcendence of any sense of self. For Jains, transcendence means self-knowledge and freedom from all worldly fetters (including, at the point of Moksha, the constraints imposed by nature). The sense of the individual's significance has contributed to Jain success, including prominence in the commercial and financial sectors. However, it is a different individualism from the form conventionally understood outside the Jain community and which, in particular, forms the basis of classical liberal thought. For individuality is believed to progress (or sometimes regress) from one embodiment or incarnation to another until the point of self-knowledge, where Moksha is attained. Physical limits are abolished, but the individual essence persists as a unit of pure consciousness. In traditionalist Jain cosmology, the enlightened being or *siddha* ('liberated soul') rises to the upper levels of the universe corresponding to the highest forms of self-realisation. The *jiva* (life monad or unit of consciousness) is the building block of the Jain cosmos. Its journey through progressive and regressive incarnations mirrors the process of expansion and contraction of the 'inhabited universe' over aeons. The journey of the jiva is ultimately circular in form in that, when it reaches its highest stage, it is also returning to its point of origin.

This process is part of the 'religious' aspect of Jain Dharma. It incorporates a variant (and, many Jains would say, the original version) of the more familiar Buddhist and Hindu doctrines of reincarnation and karma. Yet it is also a unique and intricate cosmology, which through a process of reasoned deduction was able to envisage a universe teeming with life and developed a concept of the *Anu* (infinitesimal being, either an atom or a sub-atomic 'ultimate' particle) many centuries before the invention of the microscope (Mardia 2007: pp. 35–42). The process of spiritual evolution undertaken by the jiva is at once mechanistic, as the cycles are largely involuntary, and ethical, in that the higher incarnations are more attuned to Dharma as the underlying order of the universe. Greater knowledge also confers greater control over one's destiny, which is why human intelligence brings with it the responsibility to act with caution rather than the right to exploit or dominate other species. By no means all Jains accept this cosmology in a literal sense, but it still provides the intellectual and spiritual foundations for their system of values.

Respect for life in its infinite variety is the best-known feature of Jain culture, with the exception perhaps of business acumen. For Jains, all living organisms, including animals, plants and minerals, have in common the fact that they contain jiva, the life essence. Each individual jiva is at a different level of development but is on the same journey towards Moksha. The shared possession of jiva demands mutual respect. Therefore, it follows that tolerance and acceptance should be extended as far as possible to all forms of life. Contrary to popular perception, there is no conception of equality between species. Instead, there is a hierarchy of life, viewed as a spiral moving gradually upwards, in which humans occupy the highest level of consciousness, but are also subject to the strongest ethical restraints. This notion of a complex hierarchy of species is countered by a radical rejection of human supremacy and an acceptance that species other than *Homo sapiens* possess intelligence, perception and sensitivity that matches and sometimes outclasses the equivalent qualities in humans. Thus Jain thinking anticipates the observations and conclusions of evolutionary biologists (for example de Waal 2016) about animal intelligence and ingenuity. Such ideas are radical in Western terms, but have long been taken for granted within Jain communities.

For the individual jiva, unrestrained behaviour can lead to a downward spiral away from the ultimate goal. For an entire species, it can entail extinction. The human capacity for progress is balanced by an equal propensity for regression and destruction. This attitude towards the human condition, at once deeply fatalistic and radiant with optimism, underscores Jain practices of living within the limits set by nature. A sense of the vastness of the universe, deriving from traditional cosmology and reinforced by modern astrophysics, encourages the Jains to take a long-term view of what would otherwise be everyday decisions. It also informs attitudes towards wealth and property, ownership of which is viewed as a form of stewardship for future generations, to be used in socially responsible and sustainable ways (see Chapter 5). Of equal importance is the idea that everything that contains life (jiva) has its own unique naya, or viewpoint, which is part of a larger universal truth.

For those outside the Jain tradition (including this author), this distinctive doctrine requires the shedding of many convenient assumptions about the role of the individual, the definition of community and society, and the dichotomy between transcendent spiritual experience and positive engagement with the natural world. For Jains, the quest for liberation from karmic matter and the attempt to live harmoniously with nature complement each other. The result is a way of thinking about the environment that overlaps with (and predates by a long way) modern green concerns, but also at times draws radically different conclusions.

Rationale and structure

The purpose of this brief study is to describe the environmental philosophy of the Jains, both in its theoretical basis and its quotidian observance. It identifies Jain Dharma as an ancient but highly adaptive minority culture with characteristics that set it apart from Hindu, Buddhist and other Indic philosophical or religious traditions. The principal focus is necessarily on the rational or 'scientific' aspects of the Dharma rather than its religious or mystical elements. At the same time, it recognises that for Jain communities the distinctions between philosophical speculation, spiritual practice and 'everyday life' are often blurred or non-existent. That said, Jainism will be explored primarily as a philosophy influencing secular activity rather than as a faith tradition centred upon religious ritual. In this context, Chapter 2 examines the Jain worldview in greater detail, summarising its key concepts and their points of intersection – and divergence – with Western-led environmentalism.

Chapter 3 explores the concept of karma in greater depth, emphasising the ways in which it differs from the definitions that are likely to be more familiar to Western readers especially. It discusses the relationship between the Jains' idiosyncratic interpretation of karma and the practice of Ahimsa. The connection between 'karmic accumulation' and the despoliation of the environment in the interests of economic expansion is explored in the context of interdependence: the idea that all life is 'bound together' by the karmic experience. Interdependence balances the individual's quest for self-improvement (be it material or spiritual) with his or her responsibilities towards a 'society' not limited by species.

The concept of interdependence gives rise to a form of pluralism based on mutual respect and the accommodation of differences. As noted above, everything that contains jiva or life energy has its own viewpoint or 'version of events' and is (knowingly or otherwise) part of the same quest for ultimate truth. Diverse human cultures, along with diverse animal and plant species, have an underlying unity in possession of jiva, although each jiva is itself a distinctive entity. They are united as well by involvement with karma, and although the ultimate goal is liberation, spiritual (and hence social) development involves learning to co-operate rather than exploit or dominate other living systems.

This aspect of Jain thought, which we address in Chapter 4, can seem abstruse when viewed from a secular and rationalist 'naya'. Nonetheless, the theory of Anekantavada translates into a rational code of conduct and thought. In human terms, this means acceptance of alternative viewpoints, perspectives and belief systems with equanimity, a stance that has proved highly practical for Jains throughout their history, enabling them to preserve their beliefs and culture as a small minority both in India itself and as immigrant communities elsewhere. Today, the concept of 'multiple viewpoints' is a useful tool for living in plural, multicultural societies and responding to the globalisation of politics and commerce. At an ecological level, the doctrine of many-sidedness translates into avoidance of injury to an environment composed of beings with their own naya. Once again, we examine the ways in which this approach overlaps with and differs from more familiar versions of environmental thought.

From the concept of non-injury or reduction of harm flows a practice akin to the green objective of 'living lightly'. The vow of *Aparigraha* (non-possessiveness) is based on commitment to reduce material consumption and conserve natural resources. These anti-materialist positions accompany Jain success in the commercial sector. Furthermore, as Chapter 5 reveals, they are regarded as key contributors to that success. The business model for Jain enterprises is not one in which expansion is seen as an end in itself. On the contrary, there is an emphasis on consolidation and the preservation of values (including respect for the environment) and preserving links with local communities. Small and medium sized enterprises (SMEs) are the staples of the Jain economy, and larger companies tend to share many of the characteristic features of SMEs, remaining under the ownership and control of an extended family group.

From some predominantly Western perspectives, such practices challenge the political goals of 'meritocracy' or 'equality of opportunity'. From a Jain perspective, by contrast, they prevent commercial enterprises from becoming oversized, detached from their surroundings or losing their sense of responsibility. Chapter 5 explores some of the ways in which businesses form the basis for a longstanding tradition of philanthropy and charitable giving. This giving encompasses animal welfare alongside public health and educational initiatives, including the building of schools and hospitals. Rather than implying total control, the sense of social and environmental responsibility so central to Jain daily practice stems from an idea of ownership as a form of usufruct or stewardship. Ownership of commercial or residential property, or a family business, imposes ethical constraints on the owner. Rather than having the right to expand or dispose at will, he or she is enjoined to conserve, consolidate and occasionally downsize. Entrepreneurial success is defined in terms of contraction and consolidation at least as much as growth. Whatever the size of the company, the retention of its original character and values is considered to be of the utmost importance. Ethical constraints of this kind often mirror the concerns of environmentalists and point towards a holistic model of entrepreneurship well suited to an ecologically conscious age.

Chapter 6 provides a concluding summary of why the Jain version of environmental philosophy should be of far wider interest and why the case study of Jain communities is relevant to current debates within environmentalism. It should be noted that the tenor of the book is, in the broadest sense, pro-Jain. The philosophy of the Jains is its starting point and the case is made for it as a useful and timely non-Western contribution to environmental thought, offering an intellectually coherent critique of the current model of apparently limitless economic expansion. Ideas originating in Jain Dharma will, nonetheless, be critically evaluated, while their effectiveness will be examined through (for example) specific case studies of businesses or non-governmental organisations (NGOs). Therefore, while the underlying assumption of the book is favourable to Jain ideas being taken seriously, it is not intended to serve as propaganda for these ideas.

For Western commentators, there are two prevailing positions on Jainism. The first is to view it with profound respect as an intellectual tradition and a rich culture, but to see it primarily in an historical and culture-specific context, lacking more universal relevance (Dundas 2004). The second is to idealise it, emphasising the purity of Jain doctrines and at the same time conflating them fully with the recent conclusions of Western green campaigners (Tobias 1991). There are skilful and compelling arguments in favour of both positions, but this book attempts, in a spirit that is arguably more Buddhist than Jain, to find a middle way between them. The historicist approach takes insufficient account of Jain Dharma as a living tradition. Nor does it take cognisance of the increasing need for voices from the Global South to stimulate thinking about the environment, political pluralism and a more human-scale understanding of economics. At the other extreme, the 'idealised green' position can lead to forms of cultural appropriation or *ersatz* Jain practice in the West. Equally, it can result in the superimposition of Western ideologies onto Jainism so that the latter is misunderstood or obscured from view. Jain doctrines are put into practice by people with the same range of abilities and imperfections as everyone else. Their ideals, like all other human ideals, can be neglected, forgotten or misapplied. More importantly for our purpose here, the principles of Jain Dharma are best understood when they are examined on their own merits and without Procrustean attempts to accommodate them to external prejudices or preconceptions.

Bibliography

Chakrawertti, S. (2004) 'Literacy Rate: Jains take the Honours', *The Times of India*, Mumbai (7 September 2004 edition). Also available at http://timesofindia.indiatimes.com. Accessed 2 January 2017.

Devall, B. (1990) *Simple in Means, Rich in Ends: Practicing Deep Ecology*, London: Green Print.

Devall, B., and Sessions, G. (1985) *Deep Ecology: Living as if Nature Mattered*, Layton, UT: Gibbs Smith.

Dobson, A. (2007) *Green Political Thought*, 4th edn, Abingdon: Routledge.

Dundas, P. (2004) 'Beyond Anekāntavāda: A Jain Approach to Religious Tolerance', in Sethia, T., ed. *Ahimsā, Anekānta and Jainism*, New Delhi: Motilal Banarsidass, pp. 123–137.

Fortey, R. (1998) *Life: An Unauthorised Biography*, 2nd edn, London: Flamingo.

Hofmeester, K. (2013) 'Shifting Trajectories of Diamond Processing: From India to Europe and Back, From the Fifteenth Century to the Twentieth', *Journal of Global History*, vol. 8, no. 1, pp. 25–49.

Jaini, P.S. (2001) *The Jaina Path of Purification*, 4th edn, New Delhi: Motilal Banarsidass.

Klein, N. (2008) *The Shock Doctrine: The Rise of Disaster Capitalism*, 1st edn, London: Penguin Books.

Klein, N. (2015) *This Changes Everything: Capitalism vs The Climate*, London: Penguin Books.

Kothari, J. (2004) 'A Diamond is Forever', *Jain Spirit*, Issue 20 (September – November 2004), pp. 48–50.

Lum, K. (2014, 16 October) 'The Rise and Rise of Belgium's Diamond Dynasties'. Available at: www.theconversation.com. Accessed 2 February 2017.

Mardia, K.V. (2007) *The Scientific Foundations of Jainism*, 4th edn, New Delhi: Motilal Banarsidass.

Mardia, K.V. and Rankin, A. (2013) *Living Jainism: An Ethical Science*, Winchester: Mantra Books.

Marshall, P. (1995) *Nature's Web: An Exploration of Ecological Thinking*, London: Cassell.

Meena Peters, M. (2014) 'The Remarkable History of the Diamond Trade', *Passage* (March–April 2014 edition), pp. 12–13.

Pal, P. (1994) *The Peaceful Liberators: Jain Art From India*, New York: Thames and Hudson.

Peat, D. (2006) *Blackfoot Physics: A Journey into the Native American Universe*, new edn, York Beach, ME: Red Wheel/Weiser.

Porritt, J. (1984) *Seeing Green: Politics of Ecology Explained*, Oxford: Wiley-Blackwell.

Shah, A. and Rankin, A. (2017) *Jainism and Ethical Finance: A Timeless Business Model*, Abingdon: Routledge.

Tobias, M. (1991) *Life Force: The Wold of Jainism*, Fremont, CA: Asian Humanities Press.

Trainer, F.E. (1985) *Abandon Affluence!: Sustainable Development and Social Change*, London: Zed Books.

Waal, F. de (2016) *Primates and Philosophers: How Morality Evolved*, Princeton, NJ: Princeton University Press.

2 The relevance of Jainism

> Who could ... be so superstitious as to suppose that because one cannot
> see the soul at the end of a microscope it does not exist?
>
> R.D. Laing, *The Politics of Experience and
> The Bird of Paradise* (1967: p. 19)

Jain Dharma: A summary

The interpretation of the soul articulated above by R.D. Laing, the
Scottish pioneer of radical approaches to psychiatry, is part of a
reassessment of established values and concepts throughout Western
society, a process of questioning in which environmentalism has been a
powerful component. Laing's view of the soul resembles in many ways
that of the Jains, for whom it is a hidden life principle, unique and discrete and yet connecting everything in the universe.

Jain doctrines have been transmitted from pre-literate antiquity to
the present through a series of *Tirthankaras*, or 'ford-makers' who have
liberated themselves from the cycle of *samsara*, the process of birth,
death and rebirth passed through by each jiva, i.e. each creature or thing
endowed with life. Samsara is not only the cosmic cycle of existence, but
also the process of everyday life. Liberation, for Jains, arises through
attaining the status of *Jina*: one who has overcome inner passions
and to whom material or temporal considerations no longer have any
import. The attainment of this level of self-knowledge is a springboard
towards becoming a siddha or liberated soul: the life essence rescued
from involvement with karma. A Tirthankara is a special type of siddha
whose purpose becomes the guidance of others by explicit or implicit
example. Samsara is a *tirtha* or ford to be traversed and the Tirthankaras
act as pathfinders or points of inspiration. Many Jains use them as the
focus for meditation, in some cases through images or statuary, in others
through visualisation. This is not the equivalent of worshipping deities.

Instead, it is viewing the ford-makers as inspirational examples and role models. The devotee uses them as a guide while searching within him or herself for the answers to problems in living, or at times larger spiritual questions.

Most of the twenty-four Tirthankaras are prehistoric figures whose lives are barely remembered except through fragments of hagiography. They mythical lawgiver Rishava (also known as Rishabha) is the first Tirthankara and he is recognised by some Hindus as an aspect of the deity Shiva, an example of the complex interaction between the Hindu majority and the Jain minority within Indian civilisation. Parshva, the twenty-third Tirthankara, is the first whose historical existence can be verified with reasonable reliability. He is held to have lived at some time between 872 and 772 BCE (for a full description of the life of Parshva and the mythology around him, see Zimmer 1969: pp. 181–205). The discernible 'modern' philosophy of Jainism emerged in a systematised form at the time of the twenty-fourth Tirthankara, Vardhamana Mahavira, who was born in 559 BCE and achieved *Nirvana* (full enlightenment) in 527 BCE. Mahavira means 'Great Hero', a name symbolic of spiritual victory or conquest and hence realisation of the self through non-violence and the refusal of conventional power or wealth. A contemporary of Gautama Buddha, Mahavira's path was one of more radical austerities, the origins of the vows undertaken by ascetic Jains today. This ascetic stance is balanced by the pragmatic, socially engaged and environmentally aware philosophy of daily living practised by lay men and women. Mahavira plays a supremely important role in popular Jain culture, again not as a divine figure but as a source of inspiration and practical wisdom. Many Jain households and businesses have statues or images of Mahavira and Parshva, although others view them in their more abstract form as fully realised beings, in other words as pure jiva or pure consciousness.

The traditional Jain greeting '*Jai Jinendra*' literally means 'Hail to the Conquerors'. At first sight, this has connotations of militarism and dominance, but in reality it implies the reverse. For the Jain, conquest is an internal process of self-discipline to overcome negative aspects of the self. These are principally associated with attachment, desire and 'passions' (*Kasaya*) ranging from acquisitiveness to fanaticism and doctrinaire certainty. Concepts of evil and 'sin' are not part of Jain Dharma, at least in its original form. As a rational philosophy, Jainism prefers to emphasise positive and negative developments, that is to say behaviours or thoughts conducive to knowledge and behaviours or thoughts that perpetuate ignorance. Individual conscience and individual consciousness are central to Jain theory and practice. The aim is self-realisation, which means peeling away fabricated layers of personality to understand the true self and hence the true nature of reality. This is quite different from the type of 'self-realisation' promoted in New Age or 'inspirational' books and seminars, which tend to focus on the satisfaction of immediate emotional needs or wishes. Self-knowledge involves the ability to see beyond such superficial or apparent 'needs' and view them as no more than transient satisfactions. The individual continues to exist as an independent entity after liberation from karma. This belief in the importance of the individual as a unit of conscious intelligence differentiates Jain philosophy from mainstream Hinduism and most of the Buddhist schools. It is closely connected to a commitment to pluralism (including freedom to disagree) and the importance of the individual making the best use of his or her abilities. The pursuit of scientific and verifiable knowledge is valued over uncritical adherence to doctrine, which is seen as an aid or a guideline rather than a series of set texts to be uncritically 'believed' and obeyed.

Jainism is a non-theistic system of thought, in which the workings of the universe are not attributed to any Supreme Being. It follows that each man or woman is effectively his or her own guru. Personal enterprise, individual initiative and educational attainment are all highly prized in Jain communities. Crucially, this individualism is balanced by an ethos of co-operation, whether with fellow human beings, animals, or the natural environment that sustains life. The guiding precept is a Sanskrit verse from the *Tattvartha* ('That Which Is') *Sutra* of Umasvati composed between the second and fifth centuries BCE: *Parasparopagraho Jivanam*. There are two translations for this verse: the secular and philosophical 'All life is bound together by support and interdependence' and the more explicitly religious 'Souls render service to each other'. Both translations are of equal value, but with differing emphasis. Parasparopagraho Jivanam has become a popular aphorism, signifying a belief in nonviolence and pluralistic approaches to problem solving, a pluralism that extends beyond humanity to all species. It is also the central tenet of the *Jain Declaration of Nature* drawn up by the prominent Indian jurist L.M. (Laxmi Mal) Singhvi in 2006. Written in Devanagari script, it is found at the base of the emblem adopted by all schools of Jainism in 1994 to mark the 2,500 year anniversary of the Nirvana of Mahavira, held to be the final Tirthankara for this cycle of the universe. The principle of interdependence operates at the level of friendship and family ties, community activities, business and the way Jains interact with the natural world. Vegetarianism, for instance, is considered important because it minimises harm to life: although plants contain jiva, or life essence, and possess some consciousness, it differs in degree and quality from that of mammals, reptiles or birds. Similarly, Jains are enjoined to avoid unnecessary disturbance to living organisms when constructing homes, offices, temples and gardens, or merely walking across grass.

The concept of jiva, or life monad, will be explored in more depth in the next chapter. It will be considered as part of a broader discussion of a distinctive view of karma, its place in Jain cosmology and its influence on the vows adopted by ascetics and laypeople and how these impact on philosophical approaches to the environment. Suffice for now to say that karma is, in effect, the glue that binds all forms of life together until the point of liberation. All sentient beings have in common the possession of jiva, but importantly this does not confer equal status. The samsaric cycle (birth, death and rebirth) imposed by entanglement with karma produces four *gati* or evolutionary stages of birth: *deva* ('shining ones'), *manushya* (humans), *naraki* (hell beings) and *tiryanca* (non-human animals and plants). These 'stages' are endowed with varying levels of insight, classified as senses.

Humans, along with the 'shining ones' and the hell beings, possess five senses, as do the higher primates (Jaini 2001: pp. 108–110). Animals, including mammals, birds, fish, insects and reptiles, can possess between two and five senses. Plants only have one sense, that of touch, but unlike more basic organisms 'they are distinguished by having a longer life-span and a more complex physical structure' (Jaini 2001: p. 110). Beneath all these categories (and hence outside the gati) lie several strata of one-sensed beings, the largest group being *nigoda*, who have only the sense of touch. The four gati are often represented by the *svastika* symbol, with each arm representing one of the karmic destinies. The svastika in Jain culture is also used to denote the four aspects or 'arms' of the *Sangha* (community) established by Mahavira: female ascetics, male ascetics, lay men and lay women. A symbol of light and solar energy, the svastika for Jains also symbolises the constant movement of the universe, the cycles of time and the wheel of history, including the destiny of each being.

In Jain cosmology, divine and hellish beings do not have the same significance that the terms 'God', 'devil' or 'demon' possess in Judaeo-Christian or Islamic cultures, or even 'gods' in Greco-Roman Europe. They lack either the moralistic connotations of a struggle between 'good' and 'evil' or the ability to intervene conclusively in earthly events, although they sometimes manifest special powers or 'super-knowledge' such as clairvoyance (Jaini 2001: p.110–111). Human beings possess five senses and sometimes a sixth sense referred to as mind, which is 'an integrator or input from the five senses' (Jaini 2001: pp. 121), an attribute that other five-sensed beings can occasionally attain. They are equipped with the intelligence and creativity to penetrate the illusions of karma, but they also have the power to degrade and destroy. A human gati is at once highly favourable to greater enlightenment, but it also presents the greatest risk of a form of spiritual demotion. Obtaining instruction in enlightened teachings 'can be experienced by any soul [i.e. jiva] endowed with at least five senses and a mind':

> Thus Jainas (*sic*) depict animals receiving Mahavira's teachings ... and even suggest that Mahavira himself was [spiritually and intel-lectually] awakened when he existed [in a previous incarnation] as a lion.
>
> (Jaini 2001: p. 143)

Equally, Jains 'believe that in every... state [of existence], no matter how low or simple, there will always be some residue of qualities that define the soul' (Jaini 2001: p. 111).

The hierarchy of life can be interpreted in literal or metaphorical terms by practising Jains. More usually, it is seen as a combination of both. To a sympathetic outsider to this tradition, it is an amalgam of myth, primitive cosmology and a sophisticated awareness that the Earth, indeed the universe, is teeming with elementary forms of life, all of which is significant. For Western environmentalists, especially those influenced by the secular and rationalist approaches of Western ortho-doxy, the spiritual aspect of Jain doctrine can seem arcane. Yet from it arises the insight that all forms of life are connected and that knowledge of this relationship requires (of humans in particular) responsibility and restraint. The emphasis on hierarchy, as opposed to egalitarianism, can also seem problematic, although it is balanced by a belief in pluralism and diversity that anticipates the development of multicultural societies and global communication. More radically still, the Jain worldview expresses the idea that every being, no matter how apparently 'basic' in structure, has its own viewpoint, its own value and its own role in maintaining cosmic order or environmental equilibrium.

The universalist and the exotic

In the Western imagination, there is a powerful and highly resonant image of the Jain ascetic dressed in white, his mouth covered, sweeping the ground before him with a small brush as he advances slowly for-ward. For many, this is the only impression they have of Jainism and so they form the mistaken impression that 'all Jains' live like the archetypal ascetic, rather than only those who have taken explicit and binding vows to renounce material possessions. Those who know more about the Jain community or have a wider knowledge of Indian society might also be aware of the Panjrapoor sanctuaries for abandoned or injured animals, whose lives are regarded by their carers as being as sacred as human lives. Others know of the practice of vegetarianism, viewing this diet as the defining characteristic of Jain communal life and spiritual practice. 'Jainism allows for no latitude on the subject of meat-eating' observes one admiring commentator, while 'self-defense on the part of the lay-person is, as last resort, justifiable' (Tobias 1991: p. 101). According to this literalist interpretation of Jain doctrines, a policy of militant vegetarianism overrides all other political and social considerations.

These descriptions of the Jains, like most caricatures, contain elements of the truth, however distorted and exaggerated. Only a tiny minority of Jains, for example, cover their mouths, sweep the ground as they walk or engage in ascetic practices. The male and female ascetics who live by these strict rules give dramatic expression to the underlying Jain precepts of respect for all forms of life, even the most infinitesimal. The ethical basis for this reverence for life is partly what would be broadly understood as 'moral' in a Western context. All life is sacred because it contains jiva, the life essence that has the potential for Moksha, eventual liberation or escape to the highest levels of consciousness. This 'doctrine of salvation' (Glasenapp 1999) is balanced by a pragmatic understanding that because, 'all life is bound together' (in the words of the Jain motto), forms of life that seem insignificant in the popular imagination might (in fact usually do) have hidden significance. Their welfare, in other words, might be critical to human survival or the survival of all life on earth. The shared attribute of jiva unites apparently disconnected plant and animal species in an evolutionary chain and makes them interdependent as much as they are distinctive entities. This position of scientific rationalism challenges the mechanistic worldview associated with industrial civilisation (and therefore primarily 'the West' as an economic hegemon), which emphasises individuality over interdependency, separateness over connectedness. However it also accords well with the movement (again principally in the West) away from an essentially mechanistic interpretation of science towards a holistic view based on the connections between disparate species (Fortey 1998). The universe is perceived increasingly as an 'implicate order' in which 'we must do justice to each of the parts' (Bohm 2002: p. 111) and there is a shift of emphasis towards cyclical rather than narrowly focussed linear thinking (Peat 2006). In the sensibility of 'Jainness' (see Chapter 1), the scientific and spiritual approaches to jiva enjoy a complementary relationship, or more accurately are seen as extensions of each other. Significantly, Jains have not experienced the conflict and distrust between these two ways of looking at the world that have adversely affected many other civilisations.

Jain reverence for life is subtler than literalist interpretations allow. For lay Jains, the vast majority of the population, the concept of himsa or injury is divided between *bhava-himsa*, or 'the intention to cause pain', and *dravya-himsa*, or 'the enactment of pain' (Tobias 1991: p. 58). Neither is 'worse' than the other and such moralistic terms miss the point. If anything, the intention to harm (including harm to the environment) is more serious when viewed through the Jain ethical lens, which is based on long-term thinking and reflection on the possible unintended consequences of every action. Careful Action requires careful thought and the lines between thought and activity, theory and practice are blurred in ways that are often unsettling to outsiders. Ascetics dramatise for the lay population the principles of Careful Action and Ahimsa (avoidance of harm) through behaviours that can appear exaggerated. Lay men and women, who adopt less stringent vows, attempt to integrate these practices as far as possible into their lives, by such conscious actions as adopting a vegetarian diet, but also by maintaining a sense of perspective about material possessions. Through meditation, they remember that material success is transient and illusory. Jain ethics also remind them that such success confers a corresponding increase in the obligation to 'render service'.

This viewpoint lends itself to comparisons with Western environmental concerns, especially those of a minority current of Western opinion (mainly associated with the movement known as Deep Ecology) that is engaged in questioning the received wisdom of economic growth as an end in itself. In the Panjrapoor, animals including insects are tended with care however injured or ill they might be in an apparently literal (and exacting) interpretation of Ahimsa. These institutions reflect pioneering approaches to animal welfare, both in India and globally, but at the same time they deny to sick and wounded animals the right to ultimate release from suffering, a right which Jains accord humans suffering terminal illness, who are permitted – in a sense like ascetics – to withdraw from life (Jaini 2001: pp. 229–231). Thus the Panjrapoor embody both radical ideas about the welfare of animals and the value of their lives both as species and as individual beings, and at the same time an ultra-conservative or religious view of life as inviolable whatever the level of suffering and pain involved in continuing to live. They raise the status of animals and educate the public about animal welfare, but simultaneously embody the idea of a hierarchy of life with humans enjoying a privileged role.

This conception of a hierarchy of life bears some resemblance to the idea of a 'chain of being' that was widely held in medieval and Renaissance Europe (Tilyard 1998). Unlike Jain Dharma, the chain of being was a theological concept with God as at once the head of the chain and independent of it, as well as the source of all life. Like Jainism, and unlike the mechanistic and linear approach of the West's industrial era, the chain of being acknowledged the interdependence of all forms of life as aspects of creation, but it accorded special status to human beings as having access to divine wisdom. In Jainism, where there is no creative deity or First Cause, the hierarchy of life is viewed more easily as a spiral than a chain. Yet it is a hierarchy nonetheless and differs markedly from the Western concepts of animal rights, which posit the concept of approximate equality (Singer 1975). Similarly, while the material ambitions that so often lead to despoliation of the environment are perceived as transient, so is the environment itself. The aim of spiritual practice is not to 're-embed' the self, or humanity as a whole, in the natural world, but to transcend that world and ultimately escape it altogether. Jain Dharma's relationship with the environment points in two directions, which might seem contradictory until we abandon, at least temporarily, the position of *Ekantika*: the one-sided thinking that favours either/or choices over multiple possibilities.

One of the dangers associated with the literalist interpretation of Jain practice among sympathetic Western observers is that it can create a misleading impression of Jains as permanent activists who 'stage protests' (Tobias 1991: p. 101). The culture of protest associated with sections of the environmental movement in Europe, North America and Australasia is remote from the ethos of most Jain communities and the personal priorities of most practising Jains. This is because it has emerged from a different cultural setting, framed by either/or logic and responsive to different political and economic pressures. Most Jains live in or retain close connections with the regions of the world known for convenience as the 'Global South'. In both India and East Africa (where the majority of Jain communities are still found), emergent economies are still engaging with the legacy of nineteenth and twentieth century colonialism, recovering their cultural as well as their economic confidence.

From this perspective, modernisation of the infrastructure and certain forms of economic expansion can prove beneficial both for humans and the environments on which they depend. For example, the Veerayatan movement of grassroots environmentalists in Bihar, northern India, is involved in equipping villagers with new skills, including technological capabilities, so that they can live more harmoniously with an environment brought under increasing pressure by their subsistence farming practices (Shilapi 2002: p. 166; Shah and Rankin 2017: pp. 83–85). Founded by Jain female ascetics and based on Dharmic principles, Veerayatan recognises that technological improvements and a move away from traditionally rural occupations can make human life and the ecological balance less precarious. As a result, human activity becomes less threatening to other species and their habitats. This vision of sustainability can come into conflict with the anti-technological bias of some Western environmentalists. In the West, green campaigners and thinkers are addressing the problems of an industrial (and increasingly post-industrial) society where economic expansion is often viewed as an end in itself and where environmental thought is influenced by a sense of the social and cultural loss that arises from 'over-development'.

Opposition to the ideologies of unlimited economic growth is frequently accompanied by an attitude of regret, at once social and spiritual (Sessions 1995; Snyder 1999) and hence the search for a 'simpler way' (Trainer 1985) and an idealised or romantic vision of 'indigenous', preindustrial or 'primal' societies. This attitude is partly a reaction to the specific pressures experienced by industrialised societies, in particular the widely perceived loss of shared values and a sense of community. It also arises from a mode of thought that tends to favour binary choices over multiple possibilities: Ekant in place of Anekant, to apply the language of Jain logic. Implicitly, we must choose between modern urban living and the pristine natural order, between technology and simplicity, or between the scientific-rational and the spiritual-intuitive worldviews. Jainism does not accept such dichotomies. It is possible to combine careful ecological action with economic expansion, albeit within carefully defined limits and with an emphasis on consolidation, stewardship and social responsibility. Equally, technological advances and urbanisation are not *inherently* inimical to environmental and social wellbeing. Poverty and lack of educational opportunity, as Veerayatan's grassroots campaigners understand, are the main barriers to environmental awareness. Urbanisation can increase personal freedom, including freedom from caste, class or sectarian barriers, opening opportunities to millions to fulfil their potential and improve the status of women. For Jains therefore, it is not technological and cultural changes that are themselves the problem, but the way such changes are organised and controlled and the attitude adopted by those who introduce change. To the external observer, Jainism can appear unyielding and extreme, but in practice it is a flexible philosophy of life with a pragmatic stance. Such pragmatism has enabled a minority population to play a leading – and peaceful – role in India's economic life through diverse phases of Indian history, as well as forming successful and cohesive communities in disparate regions of the world.

Those who approach Jain Dharma as outsiders and interpret its doctrines rigidly are in danger of ignoring the most significant and universally applicable aspects of Jain philosophy. With their focus on the vegetarian diet and the high status accorded to asceticism, such observers neglect the pluralist and tolerant sensibility of Jain culture. It would be inconceivable for most Jains to wish to impose their dietary practices on societies where they were culturally or climatically inappropriate. To use an extreme but illustrative example, there would be no wish to legislate for vegetarianism among the Inuit of Greenland and North America whose culture has already experienced systematic assault from Western colonialism and Christian missionary activity (Jakobsen 1999). An imposition of this kind would be wholly impractical at one level, and at another it would disrupt the efforts of Inuit communities to reconstruct a balanced working relationship with their natural environment, including sustainable fishing and hunting for food rather than sport or profit (Brody 2002). Jainism in its religious or spiritual aspect is not a 'missionary' faith that seeks converts or expects others to 'become Jains' by copying its practices and precepts. In its philosophical aspect, it does not attempt to attract narrow adherents but to offer a framework for thinking, meditating and clearing the mind of fixed ideas or prejudices.

Those who know Jain communities will have experienced a certain reticence about direct discussion of the principles by which they live. This reserved response can be interpreted as the product of an inward-looking culture. A more subtle interpretation is that their very reticence is a philosophical stance, stemming from an avoidance of doctrinaire certainty. The complex system of logic known as *Syadvada* (qualified definition) will be considered in Chapter 4 within the concepts of attitudes towards the environment and humanity's place in it. 'Syat' in Jain discourse is approximately translated as 'maybe' or 'perhaps'. It is an expression of infinite possibility. This approach acknowledges that there are many paths towards the same truth, which every human, indeed every being, is attempting in a limited way to grasp.

Jain communities are guided by a pluralist interpretation of reality that accepts many paths towards the truth, but does not reject the idea of truth itself. They face outwards, embracing possibility, but also retain an inner-directedness that enables survival and the transmission of ideas from one generation to another. Most Jain businesses are owned and run by extended families. This device ensures the continuity of the business's ethos at the same time as the family's own continuity and economic independence. The contrast between the pluralistic and self-sufficient currents in Jain society presents an apparent paradox. It is therefore possible to form an impression of Jain Dharma as a closed system that has little or no relevance except as a cultural curiosity. Paul Dundas, a British historian of Jainism, stops short of this position, but views Jain doctrines as worth examining primarily within the context of the culture and circumstances in which they have evolved. Implicitly, they lack relevance to more universal or global questions in twenty-first century society, other than those that impact directly on Jain populations. Of the Jain approach to the environment, he observes:

> Nature and its manifold qualities, seen and unseen, have no autonomous value for Jainism, but instead are linked to the various gradations of Jain epistemology, in that the more spiritually advanced the individual, the more developed his knowledge, and consequently the greater awareness he possesses of the infinite and increasingly minute constituent elements of the universe.
>
> (Dundas 2002: p. 96)

This critique of Jain approaches to the environment is based on the transcendent aspect of the Dharma: Moksha as liberation of the individual from his or her connection with the natural world. A contrasting version of liberation through reconnecting with nature is the *leitmotiv* of Deep Ecology (Devall and Sessions 1985; Devall 1990; Griffin 1984; Naess *et al.* 2010). Deep Ecology has profoundly influenced the intellectual landscape of Europe and North America in questions relating to the environment and our place within it. With notable exceptions, such as the work of Norwegian philosopher Arne Naess (1921–2009) who combined intellectual inquiry with activism, Deep Ecology has had little direct or practical bearing on the green political movement or on attempts to apply the principles of sustainability to business, in which many Jains are active participants. Despite this, it has acted as a powerful philosophical point of reference for Western-led environmental movements.

In particular, the principle of Ecological Wisdom was one of the original 'four pillars' of green politics along with Social Justice, Grassroots Democracy and Non-violence (Spretnak 1986: p. 36). It derived from Naess's concept of *ecosophy*, or humanity as part of a 'total-field image' of Nature, which closely resembles the Jain idea of interdependence. Ecosophy T, a later development in his thought, is based on the idea of self-realisation by each individual, and not just human individuals (Naess 1989: pp. 164–165). The 'T' refers to Tvergastein, a mountain hut in the Hallingskarvet range in southern Norway, where a large proportion of his writing and thought took place, in other words the place where he realised himself. The concept of self-realisation in Deep Ecology has much in common with the Jain concept of naya, or individual viewpoint as a fraction of universal truth. However, Deep Ecology goes beyond the sense that all life has intrinsic value to apply the principle of 'biocentric egalitarianism', in which all viewpoints are not merely valid but in essence equal. This essence is the subject, inevitably, of continuous distillation so that it can be applied either in practical ways through green politics (in which Naess was also a pioneer, founding Norway's Green Party in 1988) or through intelligible philosophical discussion. Deep Ecology questions the philosophical assumptions behind industrialisation and unrestrained economic expansion, labelling them *anthropocentric*, or human-centred, and advocating in contrast a *biocentric* or nature-centred approach.

The term anthropocentric is now in frequent use among environmentalists and green politicians. Unlike much of 'mainstream' green thinking, Deep Ecology aims to transcend the political boundaries of left and right: Naess (1989) advocates drawing inspiration, cultural as much as political, from Red, Blue and Yellow currents of opinion (respectively socialist, conservative or liberal) without being beholden to any of them and adopting a distinctive stance. Green parties in particular and environmental campaigners more generally tend to be allied with the 'Red' or left-wing current of opinion, in which opposition to capitalism is allied to the campaign against pollution, exploitation of the Earth and the threat to global ecosystems posed by human activities. In its simplified form, this position can be interpreted as a generalised 'anti-business' stance, bringing it into conflict with Jain communities for which commercial activities are essential to survival. The Norwegian Greens, however, remain close to Naess's position, viewing politics not as 'a question of red (socialist) versus blue (conservative), but between green and grey' (Norwegian Green Party 2017).

In contrast with the left wing of the green movement, Deep Ecology argues that state-owned or collectively administered organisations are as likely to be agents of pollution or environmental despoliation as private businesses and that the underlying philosophy is more important in this context than the economic ideology being applied. This position resonates with the Jain emphasis on multiple viewpoints and the importance of intention in determining outcomes. In a more general sense, the Deep Ecology position overlaps and intersects so closely with that of Jain philosophy that it is tempting to connect them. Yet there are two critical differences. First, the idea of equality implicit in the ecosophical view of self-realisation is distinct from the Jain concept of interconnectedness within a hierarchy of life. Ecosophy's presumption of the equality of each viewpoint obscures the idea of a transcendent truth, knowledge of which is the aim of all spiritual activity for Jains. While each naya is valid, it is only the expression of a partial truth, the reflection of individual experience. The second key difference is that, for Deep Ecologists, liberation means active re-engagement with nature. For Jains, whose aim is individual salvation through enlightened knowledge, liberation means freedom from nature's constraints, a state of being attained by a few exceptional historical or mythological figures.

Deep Ecology and its offshoot Ecosophy T are primarily intellectual movements and the subject of academic discussion. They are therefore in the background rather than the forefront of green politics and campaigning, occupying a corner (albeit a prominent corner) of environmental thought. Nonetheless, their main components have all filtered into the mainstream of environmentalist activity and thought. Biocentric egalitarianism is widely regarded as being allied to a wider commitment to social justice, with exploitation of human populations at least approximately equated with exploitation of animals, plants and natural resources. Eco-feminists draw parallels between asymmetrical gender relations, including the exploitation and abuse of women, and the abuse or destruction of the environment: anthropocentrism and patriarchy are portrayed as two sides of the same coin (Griffin 1984). Such comparisons are, in themselves, fully compatible with Jain ethics, which emphasise the relationship between all types of 'himsa' or 'harm' and recognise the continuity between exploitative human relationships and the exploitation of nature. The difference is primarily one of emphasis. For nature, according to Western environmentalists and green activists, possesses (to use Dundas's words) 'autonomous value', which humans, individually and collectively, should recognise.

Dundas's conclusions, cited above, are less a criticism of the Jain position on the environment and more a summary of the crucial difference between that position and the stance adopted by environmentalists in the West. However, implicit in his argument is a sense that Jainism's insights are ether irrelevant to or merely outside the current environmental discourse. This is because Jain Dharma is a transcendent philosophy empowered by the soteriological idea of Moksha, and because it is not (in Western secular terms) an egalitarian ideology. Furthermore, it starts with the individual, as possessor of jiva, whose goal is a return to pure, unsullied consciousness. Moreover, what we call the natural world is a manifestation of karma, the system of entanglement that binds each living being to the repetitive cycles of existence. The web of life is ultimately a trap to be escaped.

This position contrasts with the 'indigenous' holistic worldview as interpreted by supportive Western intellectuals (Peat 2006) and the conclusions of the Deep Ecologists, both of which accord primary significance to nature as it is directly experienced. Reconnecting with the natural world is a way to achieve personal fulfilment as well as working towards social and environmental justice. Such conclusions are aimed primarily, and perhaps inevitably, at well-educated and relatively affluent members of urban industrial societies. Real indigenous spirituality, although nature-centred, tends to adopt a less idealistic view of a natural world that is at least as likely to be malevolent as benign (Métraux 1972; Reichel-Dolmatoff 1997). This approach is close in some ways to that of Veerayatan, whose workers recognise that modernity can also be liberating and that technology can improve the environment for poorer communities especially. The liberating power of nature for the individual and the 'autonomous value' of the natural world have become staples of popular environmentalism in the West. The reason for this is not only the intellectual influence of Deep Ecology, but also the cultural influence of either/or logic, in this instance 'wild' or 'pristine' nature versus urban 'civilisation'.

The interpretation of Jainism as culture-specific and so of limited universal interest would seem to contrast with the parallel view of it as a radical, transformative 'movement' whose ascetic and dietary practices should be emulated by non-Jains. Both, however, make the same mistake of superimposing Western patterns of thought on the Jain experience. Recent years have seen Western 'converts' claiming to have 'become Jains', adopting names associated with Jain ascetics and claiming to be on a mission to 'spread' Jainism, usually by seeking to impose a fundamentalist interpretation of vegetarianism (Sims 2015; Flaccus 2013) and animal rights. Both the 'universalist' and 'exotic' views of Jainism start from a Western or 'Eurocentric' frame of reference, emphasising its otherness and unfamiliar or arcane practices. One response to this otherness is to consign it to a convenient 'Eastern' or exotic compartment, and the other is to embrace its outward forms and practices uncritically, extracting them from their cultural and historical contexts and attaching them to the preoccupations of Western political activists.

In the context of humanity's relationship with the environment in a globalised, increasingly 'connected' age, neither approach appreciates the potential Jain contribution. Far from being a missionary 'movement' seeking 'converts', Jain Dharma is better understood as a cultural disposition that challenges us to think about our personal and collective priorities. The process of questioning forms the core of Jain theory and practice, which are not easily distinguished in everyday life. Nonabsolutism is more fundamental than a vegetarian diet. Indeed, it is the inspiration behind vegetarianism because it arises from a reassessment of human priorities, such as the need to exert control over other species. As a form of intellectual meditation, Jain philosophy questions whether power (conferred through mental or physical strength) should justify dominance or promote the opposite stance, that of benign withdrawal. It questions us about the uses and limits of technology, our ability to overcome natural forces and our attitudes towards material possessions and the way we make use of them.

At the same time, an equally questioning stance is applied to the idea of nature as something that is inherently pure and benign that requires us to surrender. When we look beyond the outward trappings of Jain practice, we encounter a denial of absolute certainty (on the 'ordinary' human plane at least). This approach resonates with the present interconnected world where cultural values overlap and collide, where there is at once increasing unity and interaction and a revival of defensive nationalism, sectarianism and ethnic exclusivity. In this atmosphere, it provides possible strategies for mediation and compromise. The Jain system of logic can also usefully be applied to questions of human responsibility for the environment, the importance of plant and animal life, the rights and intrinsic value of each form of life, including its naya or specific standpoint.

In the latter context, Jainism's intrinsic value is that it is a non-Western philosophy in which the human response to the environment plays a central role, albeit as a means towards ultimately leaving that environment behind. Non-attachment is key to Jain practice, whether applied to possessiveness (Parigraha), partial viewpoints (Ekantika) or the idea of human dominance by virtue of intellect. A detached stance, even if only partially achieved, allows for the appreciation of life in its diversity of jiva-endowed beings.

Bibliography

Bohm, D. (2002) *On Creativity* (ed. Lee Nichol), London and New York: Routledge.

Brody, H. (2002) *The Other Side of Eden: Hunter-Gatherers, Farmers and the Shaping of the World*, London: Faber & Faber.

Devall, B. (1990) *Simple in Means, Rich in Ends: Practicing Deep Ecology*, London: Green Print.

Devall, B., and Sessions, G. (1985) *Deep Ecology: Living as if Nature Mattered*, Layton, UT: Gibbs Smith.

Dundas, P. (2002) 'The Limits of a Jain Environmental Ethic', in Chapple, C.K., ed. *Jainism and Ecology: Nonviolence in the Web of Life*, Cambridge, MA: Harvard University Press, pp. 95–119.

Flaccus, G. (2013) 'US Jains reinterpret their ascetic faith', *The Daily Star*, Beirut, Lebanon (20 August 2013 edition). Also available at: www.dailystar.com.lb/Culture/Lifestyle/2013/Aug-20/227890-us-born-jains-reinterpret-their-ascetic-faith.ashx. Accessed 12 November 2017.

Fortey, R. (1998) *Life: An Unauthorised Biography*, 2nd edn, London: Flamingo.
Glasenapp, H. von (1999) *Jainism: An Indian Religion of Salvation*, New Delhi: Motilal Banarsidass.
Green Party, Oslo, Norway (2017) 'About the Green Party'. Available at: http:// oslo.mdg.no/about-us/. Accessed 12 November 2017.
Griffin, S. (1984) *Woman and Nature: The Roaring Inside Her*, 2nd edn, Berkeley, CA: Counterpoint.
Jaini, P.S. (2001) *The Jaina Path of Purification*, 4th edn, New Delhi: Motilal Banarsidass.
Jakobsen, M. (1999) *Shamanism: Traditional and Contemporary Approaches to the Mastery of Spirits and Healing*, New York and Oxford: Berghahn Books.
Laing, R.D. (1967) *The Politics of Experience and The Bird of Paradise*, Harmondsworth: Penguin Books.
Métraux, A. (1972) *Voodoo in Haiti*, New York: Schocken Books.
Naess, A. (1989) *Ecology, Community and Lifestyle: Outline of an Ecosophy*, Cambridge: Cambridge University Press.
Naess, A. with Drengson, A. and Devall, B., eds (2010) *The Ecology of Wisdom: Writings by Arne Naess*, Berkeley, CA: Counterpoint.
Peat, D. (2006) *Blackfoot Physics: A Journey into the Native American Universe*, new edn, York Beach, ME: Red Wheel/Weiser.
Reichel-Dolmatoff, G. (1997) *Rainforest Shamans: Essays on the Tukano Indians of the Northwest Amazon*, Totnes: Themis Books.
Sessions, G., ed. (1995) *Deep Ecology for the Twentieth Century*, Boston, MA: Shambhala Publications.
Shah, A. and Rankin, A. (2017) *Jainism and Ethical Finance: A Timeless Business Model*, Abingdon: Routledge.
Shilapi, S. (2002) 'The Environmental and Ecological Teachings of Tīrthankara Mahāvīra', in Chapple, C.K., ed. *Jainism and Ecology: Nonviolence in the Web of Life*, Cambridge, MA: Harvard University Press, pp. 159–169.
Sims, L. (2015), 'Jainism and Nonviolence from Mahavira to Modern Times', *The Downtown Review* (Cleveland State University, Cleveland, OH), Vol. 2., Issue 1, Article 6.
Singer, P. (1975) *Animal Liberation*, New York: New York Review/Random House.
Singhvi, L.M. (2006) *'The Jain Declaration on Nature'* in Chapple, C.K., ed. (2002) *Jainism and Ecology: Nonviolence in the Web of Life*, Cambridge, MA: Harvard University Press, pp. 217–225. (The *Declaration* was first published in 1990.)
Snyder, G. (1999) *The Gary Snyder Reader*, Washington, DC: Counterpoint.
Spretnak, C. (1986) *Green Politics*, Glasgow: Paladin.
Tobias, M. (1991) *Life Force: The Wold of Jainism*, Fremont, CA: Asian Humanities Press.
Tilyard, E. (1998) *The Elizabethan World Picture*, London: Pimlico.
Trainer, F.E. (1985) *Abandon Affluence!: Sustainable Development and Social Change*, London: Zed Books.
Zimmer, H. (1969) *Philosophies of India*, new edn, Princeton, NJ: Princeton University Press.

3   The ecology of karma

> The operation of the body, speech and mind is action. [This] threefold
> action is the cause of the inflow of karma.
>
> Umasvati, *Tattvartha Sutra*, vv. 6.1–6.2, in Tatia (1994: p. 151)

The jiva and karma

The principle directing all other expressions of Jain ethics is that all life
is bound together: Parasparopagraho Jivanam. This motto adopted by
Jain communities across the world has a dual philosophical and religious interpretation (see Chapter 2). At the philosophical or rational
level, all life is bound together by interdependence. At a religious or
intuitive level, the jiva, as 'souls', render service to one another. The two
interpretations can be viewed as points on a continuum rather than as
separate compartments, which is why conflicts between religious practice and scientific experiment are outside the Jain cultural experience.
Loss of faith in the spiritual or transcendent aspects of Jainism need
not mean ceasing to define oneself as a Jain or withdrawing from communal rituals with religious connotations.

Thus it becomes possible for a practising Jain to view the theory of
karma, summarised above by Umasvati, as an objective truth, an elaborate allegory or a combination of both. More important than whether
the interpretation is primarily philosophical or religious is the influence
that it has over the lives and actions of Jains, as individuals, as members
of the Sangha and participants in the wider societies they inhabit. For
it is from their distinctive theory of karma that Jains derive their sense
of interconnectedness with all living systems. Furthermore, it is the
response to the challenge to karmic influence that determines their attitude to the environment and the ways in which they engage with it.

In Jain cosmology, all life is bound together, but the binding agent
is karma, acting as the glue that holds all living beings in samsara: the

cyclical process of birth, death and rebirth, which is also described as the karmic cycle. The material universe is viewed as 'a living organism, made animate through life-monads which circulate through its limbs and spheres' (Zimmer 1969: p. 227). There is no creator god or Supreme Being in Jain thought, merely a universe that is continuously changing and pulsating while retaining its essence and underlying continuity. The creative tension between continuity and change is a characteristic of Jain cosmology, which also finds expression in the ways in which lay men and women organise their lives. Dharma, after all, encompasses more than philosophical and religious speculation by human beings. It is also viewed as the natural order or correct functioning of the universe. The ethics of co-operating with fellow humans and other species stem from an acknowledgement that we are all aspects of a universal order.

Even the jiva itself expresses the tension between continuity and change. As a 'life monad', it remains constant and unaltered from the moment it comes into existence to the moment (which can be aeons hence) that it achieves liberation. However, its temporary 'mode' changes in accordance with karmic influences and the cycles of reincarnation through which it passes. Although immaterial, and in this way seeming to be analogous to the Christian idea of the soul, the jiva can also acquire karmic colorations (*leshya* or *leshyas*) arising from its embodiments and experiences. In other words, it can be 'stained' by 'association' with karma (Jaini 2001: pp. 113–114). As is often the case with Jainism, the paradox is only apparent. It is possible to envisage the jiva as eternal in its essence but transient in its manifestations, just as it is possible to view it from a scientific standpoint as a monad or unit of life, and from a religious standpoint as an eternal soul.

For non-Jains, the concept of karma can appear the most esoteric aspect of the Dharma and hence the hardest to come to terms with on an intellectual plane. Karma is an increasingly familiar word and idea for those outside the Indic traditions. Broadly, it is understood as the cosmic law of cause and effect, in which every action provokes a reaction. Karma is the law of action itself, the animating principle behind the universe. This is how it is usually interpreted within Hindu and Buddhist thought, with many other, more complex permutations. Jains also conceive of all action as a generator of karma, and as having consequences, however remote and unexpected, however large or small, for the actor and the universe. Where Jainism differs from 'mainstream' Indic thought is that it interprets karma not only as process but as substance. The pulsations of the universe bring forth new jivas: discrete manifestations of the life force within the universe itself, which is eternal and, like energy itself, can neither be created nor destroyed. Cosmic flux in turn causes the jiva to vibrate and through this activity (*Yoga*) come into contact with karma and become enmeshed in the web of life, which is analogous to the cycle of samsara. Karma consists of invisible particles (sometimes called 'karmas') that adhere to the jiva, forming a film of darkness that obscures consciousness of reality and so causing the jiva to lose touch with its original essence or true 'self'. In so far as it is visualised at all, the jiva is pictured as total clarity (the absence of colour) or pure light. The path towards liberation is seen as a journey towards the light, akin to the Western idea of enlightenment. Karmic influence, by contrast, is equated with gathering darkness.

Karmic particles consist of non-living matter (*ajiva*) in an infinitesimal form. They vary in quality and density and are attracted to the jiva by all forms of action, from the initial vibratory movement to the lived experience of the jiva's incarnations, whether automatic or consciously considered. Karmas (as these fragments of matter are often called) can be seen through the prism of modern scientific understanding as subatomic particles or 'karmons' (Mardia 2007: p. 10). The jiva is not seen as a tiny, subtle particle as in many Hindu traditions, but as a being

> pervading the whole organism; the body constitutes, as it were, its garb; the life-monad is the body's animating principle [while] the subtle substance of this life-monad is mingled with particles of karma, like water with milk, or like fire with iron in a red-hot, glowing iron ball.
>
> (Zimmer 1969: p. 229)

The 'inflow' of karmic particles, known as *asrava*, is the beginning of 'karmic bondage' or *bandha*, intimately connecting the jiva with all other forms of life. The natural tendency of karmic particles is to attract more of their number, much as ignorance deepens when it is unchecked and leads to destructive actions. Karmic bondage is at the root of the attachments that prevent knowledge of the self; indeed it can be seen as the primal attachment. Enlightenment is the gradual shedding of karma, a process that corresponds with non-violence and the dispersal of needless possessions. Listed below, the Five Vows (*Vratas*) undertaken by Jains are rooted in an ethos of social (including environmental) responsibility, but they are also a response to karma and lead to eventual freedom from all social commitments, the point at which the jiva is reconciled with itself:

- *Ahimsa*: Non-violence, non-injury, respect for all life
- *Satya*: Personal integrity, truthfulness, honesty

- *Asteya*: 'Non-stealing', avoidance of theft, taking what is not given, exploitation of human beings, animals and natural resources
- *Aparigraha*: Non-possessiveness, avoidance of wasteful consumption or unnecessary accumulation of possessions, or viewing possessions as ends in themselves
- *Brahmacharya*: Chastity, avoidance of promiscuity or exploitative relationships

Ascetics undertake the *Mahavratas* (Greater Vows) whereas lay men and women practise the *Anuvratas* (Lesser Vows). A good example of the distinction is Brahmacharya, which is interpreted as a vow of celibacy by ascetics, whereas for lay Jains it means fidelity in relationships and mutual respect between partners. The wider significance of the vow is not so much connected with sexual behaviour, or even intimate relationships, but responsible actions. Far from serving as discrete injunctions, the Vratas intersect like circles in a Venn diagram. The overarching theme is the reduction of harm (himsa) or activities and thoughts that lead to harm, whether social, environmental or personal. For individuals, the level of responsibility and social obligation increases with their levels of material success, which leads automatically to karmic accumulation. Possessions are not viewed in simple terms as a burden, but as an opportunity for both personal development and positive social activities.

Jain Dharma combines the rational search for knowledge (the scientific and literate approach) with an intuitive mentality derived from a sense of 'enchantment' and a strong identification with the natural world, with which each individual is connected by karma. The intuitive faculty 'feels' and experiences the binding together of 'all beings', identifying the process with karmic influences. Meanwhile, the rational and scientific faculty recognises the role of sub-atomic particles as building blocks of life that (like karmas) are beyond ordinary perception.

This balance accords well with the twenty-first century sensibility, including environmental concerns. Atmospheric pollution, climate change and species loss on an unprecedented scale have increased the sense that an exclusively growth-based economics is distorted and potentially dangerous. The dangers arise from a lack of sufficient reference to the conservation of resources and an interpretation of human need in terms of quantity above quality. A measure of human 're-enchantment' with the rest of nature is viewed as a welcome corrective, especially in the 'developed' world. As well as the renewal of interest in 'indigenous' spirituality noted above, scepticism about the mechanistic approach to development also contributes to the growing interest in nature-based approaches to health care (Sutherland, Moodley and Chevannes (eds) 2014; Heaven and Charing 2006). Western science has, in fact, always acknowledged the importance of the intuitive leap to scientific advance or creative inspiration. In the twenty-first century, this is perhaps reflected in a shift of emphasis from mechanical processes towards the so-called 'Eureka moment'.

From a Jain perspective, re-enchantment with nature operates at the mundane level, balanced by the idea of karma and eventual freedom from the limits imposed by nature. Yet the idea of karma does not undermine the idea of environmental responsibility. Reduction of karmic influence is based on positive engagement with society (including the environment), a policy of 'non-injury' and the gradual withdrawal from activities that impinge on fellow humans, other living systems or species. The vow of Aparigraha, or non-possessiveness, is an expression of the commitment to seeking liberation, but conserving the environment is integral to this process. The divestment of accumulated but unnecessary possessions is a radical act within what is primarily a business community, but it is regarded as a minor form of liberation, an idea to which we shall return in Chapter 5. Moreover, awareness of karma instils a long-term perspective. Planning ahead involves more than provision for immediate or extended family. Because the jiva continuously incarnates, and is embodied in a multiplicity of forms and states, everything in the universe becomes an extension of the self and a possible future.

With its definition of karma as a literal physical substance, the jiva as both a continuous unit of life and a subtle body that adapts to its surroundings, and its emphasis on the reincarnation of the jiva until the point of liberation, it is possible that Jain cosmology reflects the earliest currents of Indic thought (Zimmer 1969: p. 228, n. 48; pp. 229–230, n. 50). These have been elaborated upon in later expressions of Hindu and Buddhist thought, in which the physical idea of karma has vanished. However the archaic cosmology of Jainism is curiously in tune with today's ecological concerns and understanding of the connections between different forms of life. It has already been noted that Jains conceive of the various forms of life in hierarchical terms (see Chapter 2). In other words, they are equal in their possession of jiva, but occupy different levels of consciousness (or senses) and have correspondingly different levels of responsibility. The closest analogy is, perhaps, with the evolutionary process that connects all forms of life at varying stages of development. All sentient creatures have the possibility of working up the evolutionary spiral towards enlightenment. This is the case, however elementary the life form might appear to be, and here we should recall that Jainism, like modern science, is aware of the complexity of even the most seemingly basic organisms as well as their critical importance to the survival of life as a whole. However, 'this is not a theory of necessary evolution; the Jaina (*sic*) also accepts the possibility of retrogression' (Jaini 2001: p. 111). In this non-linear approach to spiritual development, there is no guarantee of progress towards enlightenment. An upward or downward spiral or a zigzagging through different evolutionary stages is accepted as the norm, and so evolution is not viewed as a straight line of inevitable progress.

Karma plays a critical role in the Jain perception of reality, which regards material objects and possessions as *ajiva*, that is to say devoid of life essence: they are in a literal sense 'soulless'. The process of acquiring them is therefore of transient value in comparison with protecting the living environment (everything that contains jiva). Possessiveness (Parigraha) becomes important when it acts as a destructive force, inflicting damage on the environment (including human society) and the self. Its potential for destructiveness is recognised by the vow of Aparigraha. Materialism, in the sense of attachment to possessions for their own sake, is negative from the karmic perspective. The many-sided perspective enables the practitioner to arrive at a position known as Samyak Darshana. To convey the philosophical meaning of that phrase, the most effective translation is 'correct view of reality' or 'true spiritual insight' (Jaini 2001: p. 151; p. 351). In religious practice, it translates better as 'Right Vision' or viewpoint. Samyak Darshana is a state of mind, a disposition rather than a dogmatic stance. It is based on the acknowledgement of multiple possibilities and perceptions of reality and the attempt to fuse them into a unified whole. That quality is referred to as *astikya*, which is sometimes rendered in English as 'faith' or 'belief'. It is more accurately interpreted as an implicit understanding of the nature of reality, at once intuitive and rational. Astikya is arrived at through devotional prayer with the Tirthankaras as points of reference, or meditation to achieve a state of equanimity. It is an 'affirmation' of reality, eventually giving rise to *Shraddha* or 'educated faith' (Jaini 2001: p. 151), in other words intuition reaffirmed by reason and knowledge.

A multi-layered reality is more easily visualised in terms of intersecting circles, like the Vratas or the relationship between personal, social and environmental responsibility outlined above. The 'unified' whole is therefore elusive, and so it is assumed that not every aspect of it will be grasped in its entirety. However, Umasvati's *Tattvartha Sutra*, which clarified so much of Jain thought for the lay practitioner, lists nine aspects of reality or 'things' (*tattva*) in which a clear distinction is drawn between what is real and what is ultimately false or transitory. The tattva (or 'tattvas') are sometimes known as the 'Nine Reals':

- *Jiva*: unit of life, soul, that which is sentient
- *Ajiva*: inert matter, material as opposed to living 'things', that which lacks sentience
- *Asrava*: influx of karma, obscuring the jiva's consciousness of itself (and blocking the individual's spiritual development)
- *Papa*: negative or destructive karmic influence (including negative thoughts and actions, violent fanaticism, false or misleading material attachments)
- *Punya*: positive karma (including creative or altruistic actions, benevolent or loving attachments and thoughts); Punya activities are still karmic because all actions attract karma, but they point the way towards eventual release from karmic influence
- *Bandha*: karmic bondage, or the experience of being encased in (particles of) karma and exclusively or overly involved with material concerns
- *Samvara*: stoppage of karmic influx; awakening consciousness
- *Nirjara*: breakage, shedding, falling away of karmic influence; further development of consciousness
- *Moksha*: liberation, release from karma, omniscience or full understanding of reality, understanding of the true self

Interestingly, inert or 'soulless' matter, including karma itself, counts as 'real' although it obscures our perceptions of the 'true' underlying reality. This is yet another aspect of both/and in place of either/or logic. We are not confronted with a stark choice between real and unreal, but different facets or levels of reality. Understanding the nature of reality means discriminating between what is important or necessary in the short or medium term and what is ultimately significant, between the temporary 'abode' of the jiva and its overarching purpose. Thus money and possessions, including property, are classified as ajiva or inert, but are still 'existent'. It follows that material concerns need not be ignored or treated as if they were wholly irrelevant.

Where material possessions become dominant, or are held to be ends in themselves and the governing principle of life, they become part of a 'deluded' belief system. The term *Mohaniya* is applied to the karma leading to self-delusion. Many Jains refer to the deluded state as *Maya*, deceit or illusion that stands in the way of Samyak Darshana. Maya is closely related to *Mithyatva* (or *Mithyadarshana*), false consciousness or false belief, a precursor to passions (Kasaya) and the onesided viewpoints known as Ekantika. This regressive journey is best envisioned as a spiralling downwards into karmic influence and away from enlightenment. Such regressions present special dangers to human beings and other 'five-sensed beings' (see Chapter 2) because increased consciousness also increases the likelihood of delusion.

The idea of human separation from the environment, which is then converted into a disposable resource for human use, is a form of delusion. It is also an extension of Parigraha, the sense that we 'own' our natural surroundings and that the only value they have is in monetary terms or their potential for exploitation. Aparigraha is a path towards Nirjara: the falling away of 'karmons' mirrors the disposal of wasteful or unnecessary possessions, which are then put to positive use (a form of Punya). When the process of shedding karma begins, the particles are said to fall from the subtle body of the jiva 'like ripe fruit' (Jaini 2001: p. 113). Punya is associated with enlightenment and is depicted as 'light' or 'white' karma, in contrast to Papa, which is portrayed as 'dark' or 'black'. Punya is also viewed as a physically lighter karma, yielding more easily, whereas Papa weighs the subtle body down.

Enlightenment and lightness of weight are both associated with reducing consumption and adopting a more detached stance towards the rest of the natural world, seeing it less as something to be 'possessed' or 'used' and more as a complex array of life forms and modes of existence, linked invisibly by the shared possession of jiva, the underlying life force. Recognising jiva as a form of common heritage enables the viewpoint (naya) of others – in particular different species – to be taken into account. Paradoxically, the first step towards detachment is positive social engagement. This is defined in wider terms than are conventionally used within current Western discourse. There is a powerful strain in environmentalism, for example, that is sceptical about commercial activity and regards it as inherently deleterious, advocating forms of economics that promote alternatives to private ownership, such as co-operatives, and sometimes seeking to avoid the profit motive altogether.

None of this is incompatible with Jain worldview and some Jains participate in such ventures in a practical way: many extended family enterprises are also run on essentially co-operative lines (see Chapter 5). The difference is that Jain ethics adopt a more flexible definition of social engagement. Thus commercial activity can be a positive force if it lifts communities out of poverty and promotes education, social (encompassing animal) welfare and environmental conservation. In many respects, the Jain position prefigures the idea of sustainable enterprise that recognises environmental responsibility as both morally just and economically efficient. Jain values go further, blurring or even erasing the distinction between business and charitable activity, including nature conservation. This stance is strongly reflected in the work of the Veerayatan movement (see Chapter 2), which promotes modern commercial enterprises as a way of reducing poverty. Since all activity is karmic, it is in a sense beside the point to differentiate between types of activity (commerce, conservation, charity, etc.), but more appropriate to focus on the intention behind it and the tangible results. Usually, short-term thinking, one-sided dogmatism and the refusal to acknowledge the principle of interdependence motivate harmful activities. Long-term planning that takes account of the 'binding together' of the whole physical world is more likely to produce positive results. Work that protects the environment, alleviates poverty and increases human or animal wellbeing also leads to the reduction and eventual falling away of karma. Reduction of karma is therefore synonymous with living as lightly as is practically possible.

Why karma matters

Jain cosmology depicts the universe in a human, or at least approximately human, form (Gombrich 1975: pp. 130–132). The image of 'Cosmic Man' reflects the idea that each individual is a microcosm of society – the community of all beings – and the universe itself. All parts of the *lokakasa* or inhabited universe work together, their successful interaction making the cosmos a living, unified whole. The universe as a body is the expression of the Dharma or cosmic order in a physical form. Human behaviour should be in keeping with the original Dharmic principle of respect for life in its diversity, because this ensures the smooth functioning of the universe.

In the Jain universe, each human being or sentient creature is unique, but at the same time a minute organism within the cosmic body. The devotional and doctrinal texts of Jainism are referred to as *Anga* or 'limbs', as if literally forming a *corpus* (body) of beliefs and rituals. The gigantic size of the universe as cosmic man in turn induces a state of humility, which gently restrains the sense of personal autonomy inherent in a belief system without a Supreme Being. The universe passes through cycles of time lasting for aeons, with each cycle depicted in terms of a wheel with twelve spokes. These represent twelve ages, divided in half according to the wheel's downward and upward movement. The first six are the *avasarpini*, the descending or regressive cycle, the second six, the *utsarpini*, the progressive or ascending cycle (Gombrich 1975: p. 131).

The conception of the universe as an immense organism of which we are unique but infinitesimal parts can either be interpreted in a literal or a figurative form. Importantly, from the environmentalist perspective, a highly abstract, theoretical framework is balanced by unusually strong physical imagery. Not only is the universe imagined in the form of a humanoid body, but also karma – the presence of which underscores all ethical choices made by Jains – is visualised as a material substance. In the form of subtle particles, karma adheres to the life monad, physically entraps it and obscures its vision. The life monad, in turn, responds to the presence of karma by physical movements that either enmesh it further or enable it to force its way to freedom, at which point it ceases to move at all.

For Jains, the 'web of life' is not conceived of as an essentially positive force to which we should learn to conform or yield gently (Capra 1997). Instead, it more closely resembles an actual spider's web, one of the purposes of which is to entrap. The goal of spiritual practice is escape from that web, not entanglement in it. This might seem closer to the 'Vale of Tears' perspective of early Christianity than it is to the celebratory approach to nature that most environmentalists seek to achieve. Nonetheless, it is best understood as a two-pronged strategy. At one level, the goal is liberation from all worldly attachments (the casting off of the 'mortal coil'). Yet the way to reach that level (the second 'prong') is through engagement in sustainable ways with one's surroundings. Our level of consciousness is determined by the ability to respond sympathetically to those surroundings and their inhabitants. We do this by restraining the possessive, expansionist or greed-driven impulses that threaten the habitats of other species and by taking active steps to alleviate suffering. Such actions attract positive karmas (Punya) but point us in the direction of enlightenment and the absence of karma. The binding together of life is therefore viewed in terms of both entrapment and fellowship.

In the theory of karma developed by Jains, an arcane and elaborate cosmology is paired with a practical way of living, which involves working with rather than against the grain of the natural world. Activities such as commerce, the building of homes, schools, temples and factories, are accommodated with our environment so that disruption is minimal and wherever possible enhancement is achieved. Even daily activities such as eating, walking and shopping are planned in ways that minimise harm. Ascetics interpret the Vratas as demanding the nearest thing possible to withdrawal from the world. Lay men and women are enjoined to engage peacefully with the world around them, but to live as modestly as is practically possible and limit their consumption of resources. Through an inner-directed process of reflection, the lay Jain pictures the subtle body wrestling with karma. By looking outwards, showing active compassion and also behaving with restraint, he or she sheds some of the burdens of karmic influence. From the sensibility of 'Jainness' also arises the concept of *Jiva Daya*: sympathy or identification with all life. Sympathy is acquired by understanding other points of view, and so it is to the doctrine of many-sidedness that we should now turn.

Bibliography

Capra, F. (1997) *The Web of Life: A New Synthesis of Mind and Matter*, London: HarperCollins.

Gombrich, R. (1975) 'Ancient Indian Cosmology', in Blacker, C. and Loewe, M., eds *Ancient Cosmologies*, London: George Allen & Unwin, pp. 110–143.

Heaven, R. and Charing, H.G. (2006) *Plant Spirit Shamanism: Traditional Techniques for Healing the Soul*, Rochester, VT: Destiny Books.

Jaini, P.S. (2001) *The Jaina Path of Purification*, 4th edn, New Delhi: Motilal Banarsidass.

Mardia, K.V. (2007) *The Scientific Foundations of Jainism*, 4th edn, New Delhi: Motilal Banarsidass.

Sutherland, P, Moodley, R and Cehvannes, B., eds (2014) *Caribbean Healing Traditions: Implications for Health and Mental Health*, Abingdon: Routledge.

Tatia, N. (1994) *That Which Is: Tattvārtha Sūtra (Umāsvāti)*, San Francisco: HarperCollins.

Zimmer, H. (1969) *Philosophies of India*, new edn, Princeton, NJ: Princeton University Press.

4   Diversity and unity
The doctrine of multiple viewpoints

> There is no viewpoint that is perfect and there is no science that is complete.
>
> ... [All] philosophies are imperfect although they are the glorious blocks that build the grand edifice of philosophy. ... And as there can be reality that science does not encompass, so there can be problems that are not solved by philosophy that is an endless quest.
>
> Umasvati, *Tattvartha Sutra*, v.5.31, in Tatia (1994: p. 139)

The hidden gem

We have observed already that Jains are guided by the Three Jewels or 'Triple Gem' of their faith: Right Vision or Viewpoint; Right Knowledge or Understanding, and Right Action or Conduct. Beneath these jewels, known as the Ratnatraya or Triratna, lies a fourth gemstone, hidden from view: the doctrine of many-sidedness or Anekantavada, which gives character and meaning to the principles and practices of the Jains and also connects the concepts embodied in the Five Vows. Its purpose, as Umasvati implies above, is to build upon the foundations of an unfinished 'edifice' of knowledge.

Founded on the sense that each living being (or 'soul') has its own distinctive voice and viewpoint, the doctrine of many-sidedness also reminds us of what we have in common with our fellow humans and the non-human world. It expresses the apparent paradoxes of the Jain belief system: the creative tension between continuity and change; the goal of transcendence and the practice of engaging with the world, and the equal emphasis on individual responsibility and the need for co-operation. At the same time, many-sidedness offers a way to resolve these paradoxes. This aspect of Jain philosophy is the point where all others intersect. There is a sense in which many-sidedness defines Jain Dharma and marks it out from rival 'viewpoints'. From this perspective, many-sidedness is a particular response to the unique experiences of a minority population of adherents. Finding themselves surrounded by followers of larger, more politically powerful ideologies, they become at once tolerant and defensive. In proclaiming their refusal either to seek converts or impose their ideas on others, Jain communities can appear to integrate with the outer world while simultaneously retreating into themselves.

Many-sidedness is a convenient way for Jains to face outwards and inwards at the same time, to seek integration with the wider society in which they live and work and also reinforce their separateness from it. Viewed from an alternative angle – for with this doctrine everything is about angles – Anekantavada is the feature of Jainism that has potentially the greatest universal appeal as a 'unique selling point' in the market of ideas, with (as we have already observed) particular relevance to twenty-first century concerns. How, for example, do we reconcile the trend towards global interconnectedness through economics, popular culture, technology and movements of population with a contrasting reassertion of particular interests, including nationalism, religious revivals and the resurgence of indigenous cultures? How, in multicultural societies, do we establish shared values based on mutual trust between communities with contrasting and sometimes conflicting beliefs? How do we reintegrate humanity with 'the rest' of nature and at the same time preserve (and extend as widely as possible) the advantages conferred by education, medicine and relative freedom from nature's caprices? Such questions mirror the paradoxes inherent in Jain philosophy itself. Many-sidedness offers a form of logic that is likely, if not to resolve them in full, at least to address them with a renewed clarity and relevance.

Anekantavada is the Sanskrit term for many-sidedness and is usually contracted to Anekant. It is mentioned less by Jains than Ahimsa, the guiding principle of non-injury, or even Aparigraha, the process of casting off possessive impulses and applying accumulated wealth to socially useful purposes. Nonetheless, it exerts a powerful influence over both practices. As well as being a doctrine or philosophical system, Anekant is (like 'Jainness') a sensibility, an attitude of mind that accepts multiple possibilities, the multi-layered nature of reality and the unique 'viewpoint' possessed by each form of life. The philosophical Anekant is arrived at through intellectual speculation or scientific inquiry. The sensibility, by contrast, is achieved through lived experience, not least through the conduct of business and bringing it into line with the Five Vows.

The many-sided worldview can be viewed as a form of meditation, a de-cluttering of the mind of prejudices and preconceptions likely to induce a one-sided view (Ekant) and the actions that stem from it. The aim of such meditation exercises is to achieve a sense of perspective. This can lead to the actions associated with Aparigraha, if possessive attachment is understood as a form of one-sidedness that refuses to acknowledge the temporary nature of material success. Anekant reinforces Ahimsa, for it reminds the meditator that all life has value and purpose and that the powers we enjoy as human beings are cancelled out by our insignificance within the universe. The doctrine provides an exercise in intellectual Ahimsa or a 'non-violence of the mind' (Rankin 2006: pp. 159–193). Reality, which is identified with cosmic order or Dharma, has multiple aspects with differing degrees of visibility and obscurity, manifesting or concealing themselves according to circumstance and context. The reasoning process of Anekant is popularly likened to the experience of light viewed through the facets of a cut diamond. In homage to this analogy, there is even a company in Jaipur called Anekant Diamond Products. Existence itself is composed of 'origination, cessation and persistence' (Tatia 1994: pp. 134–140). The process of reinvention is eternal, in that although individuals and objects perish, every aspect of the inhabited universe is recycled and emerges in a new form, including the cosmos itself when it enters its next cycle. The future is 'endless' and the past 'beginning-less', but nothing within that framework remains static. The 'non-omniscient person' cannot 'perceive the existent in its reality':

> At a single moment, he can be aware either of the persisting unity (*ekatva*) of the substance [or object, person, animal, plant, etc.] and the transient multiplicity of its modes.
>
> (Jaini 2001: pp. 90–91)

Anekant does not provide a key to instant omniscience, but it allows for a greater understanding of the different levels or 'modes' of reality and the balance of continuity and change that governs all aspects of existence. At the intuitive level, it creates the sense that as living beings we are 'all in this together'.

No view is perfect: The basis of Anekant

Many-sidedness is an attitude of mind or frame of reference that guides daily decision-making. It this sense, it is rooted in 'experience and realism' (Singh 2000: p. 126). The origins of Anekant are also found in complex scholarly discourses that have little direct relevance to the lives of most Jain householders but exert a powerful background influence. In much the same way as the abstruse theory of karmic accumulation translates into the practice of Aparigraha and forms the basis for the culture of philanthropy, a subtle and complex exploration of the nature of reality has given rise to a culture of tolerance. Such tolerance does not imply easy or apathetic compromise between competing ideas. Instead, it involves acceptance that alternative viewpoints deserve critical evaluation and that ideas should prevail solely because of their intellectual worth and practical utility. Anekant is an inclusive doctrine of 'both/and' in place of 'either/or'. At the same time, it is a philosophy of 'perhaps' and 'maybe' that operates through a process of perpetual questioning and qualification rather than asserting certainties or even seeking to prove 'facts'. What is invisible is as important as what can be grasped and perceived. *Anekantavadins* (proponents of many-sidedness) admit of an infinite variety of possibilities, but simultaneously emphasise the limits of human knowledge, and hence the amount that we do not and probably cannot know before Moksha.

Anekant as a concept arose out of an attempt by ascetics and scholars to explain the nature of reality, whether visible or invisible, finite or eternal. The result of these speculations was 'a denial of absolute existence or absolute impermanence' (Tatia 1994: pp. 134–140). Thus existence is neither a continuous state of flux nor a state of rigid immutability. It is changing all the time and these changes are reflected in continuous cycles of progress and regression, expansion and contraction, decay and renewal. This process of change is balanced by a continuity or underlying stability that is of equal importance. A person or an object might change with age and surrounding conditions, but retains an enduring identity as that person or object. This example is only partially effective, because the human 'person' eventually dies and the natural or crafted object can erode, decay or be destroyed. Continuity in this context is not 'eternal' as it is with the life principle that unites us and at the same time makes us distinct. In the case of the jiva, the animating principle of continuity moves from one embodiment to the next until the point of escape from karma when it continues to exist in an unadulterated form. In so doing, it affirms the connections that bind together everything in the natural world.

This view of reality corresponds to the cyclical conception of time and the idea of the universe passing through progressive and regressive cycles. That which is real (tattva) has two aspects, the eternal and the non-eternal or transient. It is permanent 'with respect to its essential substance and impermanent with respect to [the] modes [of existence] through which it is ceaselessly passing' (Tatia 1994: pp. 134–140). One 'mode' (that is to say a phase or aspect of existence) can be 'grasped at the expense of others'. The 'grasped mode' is 'brought to light' while other attributes remain in the background (Tatia 1994: pp. 134–140). Here we can draw partial parallels with more familiar forms of dualism, such as the polarities of Yin (darkness, nurturing, contraction) and Yang (light, activity, expansion) in Daoist and other classical Chinese thought (Cooper 2012; Cooper 1981). In Jain cosmology, there are similar creative shifts between solidity and flux, but with an emphasis on multiplicity rather than duality. Several propositions can be simultaneously regarded as 'true', not because they represent the 'whole truth', but because they reflect varying aspects of reality.

It would be easy to confuse this approach with a form of extreme scepticism that accepts all modes of thought as equally valid. In fact, *Ajnanavada* or scepticism is explicitly rejected by the *Sutrakrita* (or *Sutrakritanga*), the second Anga (limb) of the Jain canon as one of the paths 'opposed to the Jina'. The other paths, also described in unequivocal language as 'wrong' or 'false', include *Nijativada* (fatalism), *Akriyavada* (non-action), *Samkhya* (eternalism) and *Charvaka* (annihilationism: the idea that there is 'nothing beyond the senses' and so only material beings and objects exist). All of these are versions of *Ekantavada* (or Ekantika), one-sidedness, and are 'thus inferior to the comprehensive (*anekanta*) Jaina view of reality (Jaini 2001: p. 53). The *Stotras*, a series of poetic hymns to the Jinas, also criticise 'ekantavadins' who 'hold absolutist doctrines' and are therefore opposed to the 'doctrine of manifold aspects' (Jaini 2001: pp. 85–86).

Here there is an apparent contradiction between the acceptance of 'manifold aspects' and the rejection of competing doctrines as 'false'. This reasoning is especially alien from the perspective of those schooled in conventional Western logic, which tends to favour making a choice between opposing versions or aspects of the truth and to stress the importance of consistency. Alternatively, it aims to combine elements of contradictory propositions into a synthesis, which is viewed as a more complete version of the truth. Advocacy of many-sidedness, by this reasoning, is inconsistent with regarding some doctrines or philosophical approaches as erroneous. Many-sided reality, moreover, does not seem so much to be a synthesis as a kaleidoscopic or psychedelic vision of reality. To understand Anekant, it is necessary to abandon the preconceptions implied by a narrow search for consistency. For falsehood is held to arise not from a 'false' idea or proposition itself, but from the refusal to acknowledge other aspects of reality and to embrace a closed system of thought. A fatalistic position, for instance, fails to take account of the importance of individual or collective endeavour. At a social level, it tends towards promoting apathy and discouraging constructive reform. Open-ended scepticism is held to undermine the sense that there are absolute truths such as the centrality of Ahimsa.

Non-action is the state enjoyed by liberated souls who are depicted in Jain iconography as seated at the top of the universe, having floated there as soon as they are released from samsara. For the 'non-omniscient' person or being, however, the failure to act (and think carefully before, during and after each action) blocks the quest for knowledge and also prevents the accretion of positive karmas. Non-action is therefore the opposite of Careful Action. Similarly, the definition of 'eternalism' (*Samkhya* or *nityavada*) as a form of false consciousness would seem to contradict the idea of the universe as eternal, the product of energies that can neither be created nor destroyed. Yet eternalism in this context is defined as the belief that only the 'substance' or material aspect of a being or an object really exists, thus denying the 'modal aspect' which is insubstantial and can transfer from one incarnation to another. Its opposite, *nityavada* or non-eternalism, denies the literal existence of substance, *dravya*, accepting only the modal or transitory aspect as real (Jaini 2001: p. 92). This line of reasoning was associated (with some degree of accuracy) by early Jain scholars with Buddhism of the Theravada school, which today predominates in Sri Lanka, Thailand, Cambodia and Burma/Myanmar. The 'denial of substance', according to Jain logicians, 'makes it impossible ... to explain logically either bondage by karma (*samsara*) or the release from this bondage (*nirvana*)' (Jaini 2001: pp. 92–93).

Such arguments could be said to resemble the disputes that characterised early Christianity (Williams 2002). They arguably continue to play as important a role in Jain thinking today as in the age of Mahavira. The quest for knowledge is interpreted as a search for completeness, an effort to put together a universal jigsaw when many of the pieces are missing or hidden from view. The existence of missing pieces compels an element of doubt based on awareness of the partiality and incompleteness of human knowledge (impeded by karma). From the premise of partial or qualified definition emerges the way of thinking known as *Syadvada*. The word *syat* in Sanskrit means 'might be', which is why Syadvada is at times referred to as 'maybe-ism'. For Jains, it is used to convey the idea of 'in some respect' (Jaini 2001: p. 94). Syat is further qualified by the word *eva*, literally meaning 'in fact'. In the context of Syadvada, the use of 'eva' conveys the 'fact' as experienced by the speaker or writer, as opposed to alternative naya or interpretations:

> Thus the statement 'the soul is eternal', when read with syat and eva would mean: 'In some respect – namely, that of substance and not of modes – the soul is in fact eternal'. By qualifying the statement in

this manner, the Jaina (*sic*) not only makes a meaningful assertion, but leaves room for other possible statements (for example, 'it is not eternal') that can be made about the soul.

(Jaini 2001: p. 94)

The soul (jiva or life monad) is eternal in that it never ceases to exist and so its 'substance' remains. However it changes its 'mode' with the character of karmic influence it experiences and the cycles of incarnation through which it passes. It is, like everything in the Jain universe, at once permanent and impermanent, static and adaptive, depending on context. Syadvada is a way of navigating between competing or sometimes conflicting nayas, not by merely conceding an argument but by admitting that multiple perspectives can coexist and that any proposition can be viewed from two or more angles:

> The spirit of this approach guards [the practising Jain] at all times from extreme viewpoints. ... Jainas (*sic*) are encouraged to read extensively in the treatises of other schools [of thought] ... It also seems likely that the failure of any doctrinal heresy to appear during nearly 3,000 years of Jaina tradition can be largely attributed to this highly developed critical analysis and partial accommodation.
>
> (Jaini 2001: p. 96)

There is a cyclical relationship between Syadvada and Anekant. The constant application of 'syat' and 'eva' induces a mood of eternal questioning and a consequent refusal to dismiss alternative views. The belief in 'many paths' towards the same ultimate goal of understanding reality fosters a spirit of inquiry and self-examination. It also, crucially, encourages an attitude of intellectual modesty. This helps us to understand why, as Padmanabh S. Jaini suggests (*op. cit*, p. 96), there has been no 'heresy' or radical schism in Jainism since its emergence as a distinctive spiritual tradition. There are two main 'schools' of Jain practice, the *Svetambar* ('white-clad') and the *Digambar* ('sky-clad'): in the case of the former, the ascetics (male and female) wear white whereas the latter's most senior male ascetics practise nudity. The Digambar Jains are, arguably, somewhat more rigorous and uncompromising in their practice, but the two schools accept each other's differences without regarding themselves as rivals and often share facilities, especially in the Diaspora. Within both Digambar and Svetambar traditions, there are also differing modes of thought following different practices or customs (for example those who use icons as meditational tools and those who reject their use), but again there is no sectarianism, but merely a pragmatic agreement to differ.

The spirit of questioning also induces a modesty in Jain communities, which is reflected in the absence of a missionary tradition and an attitude of equanimity towards cultural practices or attitudes that they might find uncongenial. Furthermore, the mental processes of Anekant and Syadvada, and the general disposition of syat/eva encourage an attitude of respect for the environment, despite not being associated with the more explicitly environmentalist areas of Jain philosophy. Careful thought becomes part of the practice of Careful Action. Treading lightly at the intellectual level serves as a reminder to 'live lightly on Earth' (Schwarz and Schwarz 1998), respecting the nayas of animal and plant species and recognising human dependence on them. Anekant, in short, has ecological implications because it influences the way in which Jains relate to their surroundings, plan their lives and view society as more than a collection of individual human beings.

'How can we...?': The implications of many-sidedness

In the United States, the Green Party of California expresses its key values in the form of questions. The principle of Ecological Wisdom, for example, prompts supporters to ask, among other things: 'How can we operate human societies with the understanding that we are part of nature, not on top of it?' 'How can we build a better relationship between cities and countryside?' and 'How can we guarantee the rights of non-human species?' Grassroots Democracy, another key value, invites questions such as 'How can we develop systems that allow and encourage us to control the decisions that affect our lives?' and 'How can we encourage and assist the 'mediating institutions' – family, neighbourhood organisation, church group, voluntary association, ethnic club – to recover some of the functions now performed by the government?' The section entitled Postpatriarchal Values encourages us to ask: 'How can we replace the cultural ethics of dominance and control with more co-operative ways of interacting?' 'How can we encourage people to care about persons outside their own group?' and 'How can we learn to respect the contemplative, inner part of life as much as the outer activities?' The other key values are Non-Violence, Social Justice, Decentralisation, Community-Based Economics, Respect for Diversity, Personal and Global Responsibility, and Sustainability (Radical Middle 2017).

Rather than serving as a substitute for policy-making, this interrogative process serves as the preamble to a more detailed programme. In the context of American third party politics, California's Greens have had a measure of success at the ballot box, electing mayors in a wide range of communities located for the most part in northern and rural areas of the state and exerting a cultural influence that exceeds their polling figures. This marks a noticeable difference from the Green parties of Europe, which have been primarily urban movements, whose supporters sense that they are disconnected from the 'natural world' outside the city and are responding to the pressures of pollution and overcrowding on the quality of their lives. Many Californian Greens, by contrast, have been influenced by the counter-culture of the 1960s, out of which in the subsequent decades evolved significant interest in alternative approaches to economics and spirituality. This gave rise to a 'back to the land' movement expressed through rural communes and distrust of centralised authority, whether political, corporate or technological (Rorabaugh 2015: pp. 205–227).

Asian philosophies have exerted a powerful and lasting influence over the counter-culture and its political manifestations, both directly and by osmosis. The civil rights movement, with its techniques of non-violent opposition to racial and social injustice, owes much to Mahatma Gandhi's *satyagraha* (truth struggle) against British colonial rule. The Mahatma, a Gujarati Hindu, was influenced in turn by a Jain merchant-philosopher, Shrimad Rajchandra (Shah and Rankin 2017: p. 95). Rajchandra encouraged him to consider the value of Ahimsa and use it to address social inequalities, including those arising from caste discrimination, since inequality and discrimination were themselves forms of violence or himsa. Gandhi's economic model for India, *swadeshi*, was based on local production for local needs and a system of economics that served the whole of the community rather than centres of affluence and political power (Rankin 2010: pp. 134–135). Importantly, the village was viewed as the centre of the economic order, drawing upon and modernising traditional structures such as the extended family and the community 'bound together' (in Jain terms) by shared values. Technology was to be on a human scale and attuned to the environment: the spinning wheel became a symbol both of sustainable technology and economic self-sufficiency. The Sanskrit word *swadesh* means 'own country', with 'swadeshi' denoting 'of one's own country'. This was part of a resurgence of national consciousness, but at the same time it pointed towards an ideal and an aesthetic associated with self-sufficiency, individual and communal responsibility, simplicity of clothing and lifestyle. Such concepts were later to be embraced with vigour by the counter-culture in North America, Europe and Australia (Roszak 1995) and underlie the key values of the California Greens and the questions stemming from them.

The long-term significance of the California Greens' approach has yet to be seen. It offers a useful example of how many-sided logic might be applied to a political discourse largely characterised by adversarial positions and doctrinaire certainty. By using the technique of questioning, it is possible to blur the conventional (and unsatisfactorily simplistic) divisions of 'left' and 'right' and find unexpected common ground with those who would usually view political and social issues from different perspectives. In the case of the Greens, it helps to explain why, their background in left-wing campaigns and the counter-culture notwithstanding, they have been able to garner support in some of the state's most socially conservative rural regions. Another partial explanation is that numerous supporters of the counter-culture settled in these areas as part of a reaction against urban life: their story of gradual and sometimes difficult assimilation also illustrates a 'many-sided' convergence of radical and conservative worldviews, as the incomers and established communities lived together, worked together and influenced each other often in subtle and unplanned ways (Rorabaugh 2015: pp. 205–227).

The political landscape in which the ten key values arose is very different from that in which Anekant and Syadvada evolved and there is no conscious connection between them except for the indirect 'Asian' influences cited above. That said, the resemblance is striking and stems from the recognition that an attitude of questioning is a more practical response to increasing complexity in economics, the environment and technology than adopting absolutist positions. Jains in India, and later in disparate immigrant communities, formulated the doctrine of many-sidedness as a survival mechanism as an exercise in speculative thought. As members of a minority culture jealous of its distinctive identity and yet highly engaged with the outer world in trade and the professions, they have been involved in a process of perpetual negotiation. In a world of increasing cultural convergence, and at the same time heightened awareness of cultural distinctions, the methodology of Anekant is worth considering outside its original Jain context.

Nowhere, perhaps, is the logic associated with 'how can we' more relevant than in humanity's relationship with the environment. Anekant is not an environmental philosophy in the restrictive sense, but part of a view of society that encompasses all living beings, not just humans, and thus reintegrates humanity with nature. Furthermore, the idea that all forms of life have their own viewpoint that is worthy of respect and has its own 'intrinsic value', irrespective of its relationship with humankind, accords with the Deep Ecology platform enunciated by Arne Naess and George Sessions, which also includes the proposition that 'Richness and diversity of life forms ... are values in themselves' which are 'independent of the usefulness of the nonhuman world for human purposes' (Naess and Sessions 1984). Although it engages positively with Asian and Native American philosophies, Deep Ecology is rooted in the Western cultural canon. It is at once a development of and a reaction against the principles of the European Enlightenment and the assumptions of industrial society. Re-engagement with nature is its goal, 'rather than adhering to an increasingly higher standard of living' (Naess and Sessions 1984). For humanity and the rest of nature, over-development has iniquitous social and environmental effects, including psychological and spiritual malaise.

Like Anekant, this form of Western environmental philosophy aims to redress the balance between humanity and the natural world. Anekantavadins, however, approach environmental issues from a perspective that differs from that of Deep Ecologists and other Western environmentalists. They operate within the framework of Jain Dharma, the faith-based aspect of which has the goal of escape from the natural world, along with all material attachments, which are manifestations of karma. Return to nature in an idealised form is not compatible with this aim. Jain ascetics, who come closest to the ideal of material renunciation, are not seeking to be 'at one' with the natural world but to escape as far as possible its demands, for they do not draw a (Western-style) distinction between nature and the material demands of urban living. Nor do those lay Jains who actively attempt to incorporate Anekant into their daily lives. Unlike Deep Ecologists, they do not idealise nature but are all too aware of its imperfections and vicissitudes. They balance the concerns of Western environmentalism about over-development with the concerns of the Global South about equitable division of resources.

The work of Veerayatan, described in more detail in Chapter 2, includes both environmental and technological education in its poverty reduction programmes for rural Bihar. This many-sided approach accepts that nature, in particular natural disasters, can be a major contributor to poverty. Education and the sensitive application of technology improve understanding and management of the environment, making natural disasters less likely. The accoutrements of modern living, such as running water and homes that withstand the elements, improve the quality of life as much as access to the natural world. This stance derives from an avoidance of either/or dichotomies. Although loss of attachment is the ultimate goal, it is recognised that poverty and underdevelopment create attachments rather than erode them. This realisation informs the Jain attitude towards business and its relationship with environmental ethics.

Bibliography

Cooper, D. (2012) *Convergence with Nature: A Daoist Perspective*, Totnes: Green Books.

Cooper, J.C. (1981) *Yin and Yang: The Taoist Harmony of Opposites*, Wellingborough: The Aquarian Press.

Jaini, P.S. (2001) *The Jaina Path of Purification*, 4th edn, New Delhi: Motilal Banarsidass.

Naess, A. and Sessions, G. (1984) 'The Deep Ecology Platform', Foundation for Deep Ecology. Available at: www.deepecology.org/platform.htm. Accessed 1 September 2017.

Radical Middle (2017) 'Ten Key Values'. Available at: www.radicalmiddle.com/ten-key-values.htm (of California and some other US Greens). Accessed 12 December 2017.

Rankin, A. (2006) *The Jain Path: Ancient Wisdom for the West*, Winchester: O Books.

Rankin, A. (2010) *Many-Sided Wisdom: A New Politics of the Spirit*, Winchester: O Books.

Rorabaugh, W.J. (2015) *American Hippies*, New York: Cambridge University Press.

Roszak, T. (1995) *The Making of a Counter Culture*, Berkeley: University of California Press.

Schwarz, W. and Schwarz, D. (1998) *Living Lightly: Travels in Post-Consumer Society*, Charlbury: Jon Carpenter.

Shah, A. and Rankin, A. (2017) *Jainism and Ethical Finance: A Timeless Business Model*, Abingdon: Routledge.

Singh, R. (2000) 'Relevance of Anekānta in Modern Times', in Shah, N.J., ed. *Jaina Theory of Multiple Facets of Reality and Truth*, New Delhi: Motilal Banarsidass.

Tatia, N. (1994) *That Which Is: Tattvārtha Sūtra (Umāsvāti)*, San Francisco: HarperCollins.

Williams, R. (2002) *Arius: Heresy and Tradition*, Grand Rapids, MI/Cambridge: SCM Press.

5 Careful action

Jain businesses and environmental ethics

> Purity of business activity is the basis of Dharma.
> Ratnaśekhara Sūri, 'Light of Purity of Business Activity'
> (Jain text from first half of fifteenth century CE)

Requiring minimum harm

In the opening chapter, the example of Vardhaman Gems illustrated the way in which the values associated with a business are not only considered 'more important' than its profitability but also perceived as an essential ingredient of commercial success. Business itself, when it adheres to a strict but pragmatic ethical code, is (as the text above indicates) viewed as part of the natural order of human society. The idea that a company should have to 'choose' between ethics and profit is, in terms of Jain logic, a contradiction in terms. Refusal to choose can be puzzling to Western observers, who come from a culture where profit is vigorously pursued and yet it remains morally ambiguous. The Jain position, entrenched by centuries of experience as a trading culture, anticipates the modern concept of sustainable business. Ecological ethics combined with practical action to protect and nurture the environment have always been viewed as indicators of economic efficiency as well as improving the quality of life.

Within Jain communities, the business ethic is not explicitly 'environmentalist', but care for the environment underlies the principle of avoiding harm to all forms of life. The jeweller pursues his trade with confidence because its processes are alparambhi ('requiring minimum harm') and so compatible with the Anuvrata (Five Lesser Vows) undertaken by Jain laymen. His task is therefore to ensure that the trade remains as free from harm as possible and that the ethos of his business is maintained as it adapts to modern technology and an expanded client base. Vardhaman Gems, for example, is now a global business but is still run by the same family and operates according to principles developed in the fourteenth century. Its guide, the *Ratnapariksha* (Gem Inspection Manual), is at once a trade manual and a spiritual text (see Chapter 1).

The *Ratnapariksha* is an example of the way in which Jainism does not draw distinctions between spiritual needs and commercial activity, long-term planning and profit in the present. Long-term planning is hardwired into Jain thought and an important part of daily life. The theory of karma emphasises the possible unintended consequences of any action, however small. It does so with greater intensity than other Indic traditions, because Jains see karma as substance that binds and accumulates. They also distinguish between light 'karmas' that point towards eventual liberation and 'heavy' karmas that point towards states of confusion and ignorance. Each action should be considered in terms of its internal effects on the spiritual development of the individual and its external effects on the environment, including future consequences that cannot easily be foreseen. The admonishment to act with care applies especially to commercial decisions because they have material consequences and, in karmic terms, material attachments are among the most dangerous delusions.

Ethical constraints on Jain business activity are therefore considerable but importantly are not absolute. Whether the businessman or woman believes literally in karma, he or she has a powerful cultural incentive towards caution. The idea of treading carefully is ingrained. We have already referred to the powerful influence exerted by the ascetic who calculates every step to avoid injury to the most minor organisms. Living as a mendicant or inhabitant of a monastery, and therefore outside the requirements of the householder, he is able to enact in a literal form, the principle of Ahimsa. This means refraining from all unnecessary actions, because even the smallest act might cause harm or have a karmic impact of some kind. It also means renouncing material possessions and so avoiding both the psychic damage created by Parigraha (possessiveness or acquisitive thinking) and the harm to other (including the environment) that the process of accumulating wealth can bring. The centrality of Ahimsa, the first and foremost of the Vrata, is the distinguishing feature of the Jain way of life. It is a yardstick against which all activities are measured, with thoughts counted as forms of activity.

While the term alparambhi is restricted largely to occupations and trades, the concept of 'requiring minimum harm' reflects the day-to-day behaviour of observant Jains. When they apply this principle to the effects of commercial activity, it has a profound bearing on attitudes towards protecting the environment, both for the present and for future generations. The goal of minimising harm requires avoidance of exploitative relationships, whether with fellow humans (including workers or employees), animals or natural resources, many of which contain jiva. In this context it is worth noting that the existence of ascetics as role models creates a sense of perspective for the entrepreneur or business owner. Material achievements pale into insignificance measured against the ideals of renunciation and non-attachment.

There is another reason why Jain businesses do not distinguish between strategies to increase viability and profit and policies to reinforce underlying values. The concept of profit differs from the conventional wisdom that unlimited expansion is in itself a measure of success. From their perspective, 'success' is defined as a balance between generating wealth and generating positive karma (Punya) through constructive use of that wealth. In addition to provision for family members, Punya is generated through positive works ranging from animal sanctuaries to schools, hospitals, research institutes and temples. The community of ascetics is also maintained by support from private individuals and families, many donating some of the proceeds of commercial enterprises. Profit is assessed as those actions most likely to ensure the continuity of the enterprise in a way that maintains its character and values: the family members are intended to serve as ethical stewards ensuring that those standards are maintained. Thus the commercial and the spiritual realms are intertwined. The latter informs social attitudes towards the former, and also influences the conduct of activities connected with material possessions.

The Jain view of ownership is one of partial detachment rather than the absolute control associated with the Western-derived model. Property, including businesses, commercial and inherited income, is essentially 'borrowed' or held on trust. Borrowing might take place over several generations, as in the ownership of a family firm, but still is not perceived as ownership in a final, absolute sense. This concept of borrowing is usually based on a shared perception on the part of the owner and his dependants, including family members, employees and apprentices. However, it can be expressed and given extra strength through formal legal contracts. As a globally dispersed community, Jains work within a range of legal frameworks governing property, land and business ownership. They have proved themselves highly adaptable to such variations perhaps because of the capacity, induced by their faith, to be detached, dispassionate and respectful of the cultural conditions in which they find themselves. Their concept of borrowing is ethical more than legalistic. It is concerned with the obligations that property ownership and business ownership impart.

Attitudes towards ownership derive ultimately from the 'Nine Reals' (see Chapter 3) and more immediately from the vows of Jain practice: non-injury; avoiding exploitation of people, animals and natural resources; the charitable dispersal of unnecessary possessions; and transparency in commercial dealings. That last quality is an aspect of the vow of Asteya, which means maintaining personal integrity as well as mere avoidance of dishonesty and theft. Anekant (many-sidedness) reminds the lay person engaged in commercial activity that other points of view are worth taking into consideration. To do so can bring good financial yields rather than compromising the business. The ascetic ideal of total renunciation remains in the background as a constant reminder that there is an alternative to material goals.

Far from repudiating the idea of economic growth, Jain culture embraces it and many businesses have made successful and lasting contributions towards their local economies. Nonetheless, a typically Jain form of business planning aims to balance that growth with consideration for social and ecological issues. Expansion is followed by a period of consolidation and where necessary contraction, to preserve the original character of the business or prevent it from being swallowed up and transformed by larger corporate entities. Responsibilities to community and environment are not regarded either as optional extras or necessary but subordinate additions, but as integral to the business's effective operation. Jain philosophy and its practical expressions are by no means unique in this sense, but they are especially stringent in their call for a sense of detachment and a long-term view. As such, they are a useful point of comparison and contrast with the prevailing business model, which for convenience we shall refer to as Western although it is no longer exclusive to the West or Global North.

Jain model

- Ownership confers responsibility towards community, society (including humans, other species and the environment)
- Presumption of stewardship of the commercial enterprise; avoidance of practices which generate harm, whether to humans, animals or the natural world
- Emphasis on self-governance: acceptance of personal responsibility as owner or manager, including responsibility for conserving natural resources
- Presumption in favour of consolidating rather than expanding: expansion can take place for pragmatic reasons but should not become an end in itself
- Balance of continuity and change: excessive conservatism leads to stagnation, but uncontrolled change results in loss of integrity and possible instability for the business
- Focus on personal relationships and community projects, including environmental and animal welfare

Western model

- Ownership confers inalienable rights
- Presumption of control: environmental and community concerns are important, but they are 'add-ons', subordinate and possibly detrimental to 'pure' commercial interests
- Emphasis on personal autonomy and self-reliance
- Presumption in favour of expansion and growth as agents of progress
- Change and flux valued over stability and continuity
- Focus on systems, 'teams', structures and bureaucracy rather than personal relationships

Jain business ethics are founded on the presumption of self-restraint and on the concept of wealth generated by an enterprise as social capital rather than exclusively for personal or familial use. As such, the generation of wealth corresponds to the generation of positive karma. Commercial activity thereby becomes a means of personal and social transformation, the 'self-conquest' to which both spiritual and temporal activities are directed. The social aspect of this process involves philanthropic and charitable enterprises, spreading outwards from the extended family towards local, national or sometimes global concerns. The concept of social, as we have noted, encompasses far more than merely human. Animal sanctuaries founded or sponsored by business are viewed as social enterprises in exactly the same way as philanthropic agencies directed at humans.

For sympathetic outsiders, such insistence on equivalent status can be disconcerting, but it derives from the concept of jiva as the animating principle that unites all sentient beings. Each being that possesses jiva is working, at some level, towards the same goal of transcending karmic ties. It is here where the social and personal aspects of Jain philosophy overlap, for Jainism is ultimately a doctrine of personal salvation. In its metaphysical form, that means self-knowledge, part of which is moving beyond all material preoccupations and ties. At the mundane level, it imposes an obligation to disperse personal power, including personal wealth and the fruits of economic success. Wise use of these resources for the benefit of others is part of the personal journey towards liberation.

Of equal importance, in this context, is acquiring an awareness of when to end the processes of accumulating wealth and expanding the business. This involves tuning in to the local environment and assessing the ecological footprint caused by commercial activity. 'Ecological Footprint' is not a term generally used by Jains in the context of business management, but it can reasonably be argued that the vow of 'careful walking' is a precursor to the idea of assessing and measuring the environmental impact of human activities.

For the Jain business model, small and medium-sized enterprises (SMEs) are at once the starting point and the point of return. As the business expands, it aspires towards a process of consolidation and even contraction, which frequently means the retention and enhancement of specialist skills and client loyalties. At its largest capacity, its point of reference is less the 'faceless' corporation and more the locally based, community-centred and family-owned enterprise. Growth is not defined solely by size or scale, but in terms of retaining core values and applying them with increasing effect and scope. Expansion can enable those values to be implemented on a larger scale, but contraction permits a return to the firm's original base. In the creative tension between expansion and contraction, commercial survival and financial acumen are highly prized, both as 'life skills' and because of the (karma reducing) social obligations they bring. Wealth is valued as a means rather than as an end.

This organic, cyclical model has worked for Jains in disparate parts of India and the world. It is governed by the need to avoid activities that do direct or indirect harm. In our discussion of the jewellery industry (see Chapter 1), we noted that Jains are involved in gemmology, valuation, sale and design in preference to the extraction of gemstones, which can disturb small organisms and create areas of pollution. The obvious criticism of this position is that Jains sometimes let others do their 'dirty work'. This charge is valid, but for Jain businessmen and women it is offset by the energy and creativity devoted to non-violent commercial activities (including jewellery) and the emphasis placed on voluntary work to alleviate unintentional harm.

Jain ethics include no in-built prejudice against trade and commerce. Nor is there any sense that commercial activities are less worthy of respect than intellectual pursuits or manual work. Because every action is regarded as karma inducing, the value of an activity is measured almost exclusively in terms of its results. There can be constructive and creative industries, as opposed to those that are liable to disrupt or pollute the landscape. In the same way, some intellectual activities enrich our scientific knowledge, artistic perceptions or human compassion, while others point us towards destructive attitudes and acts. The lack of caste-based restrictions or prejudices in Jain Dharma opens up choices and possibilities. This helps to explain why a small population, such as the United Kingdom's less than 40,000 Jains, has nurtured such a varied range of commercial enterprises.

The case study we shall consider below, from the pharmaceutical industry, would seem an unusual choice from the perspective of environmentalist orthodoxy. However, the principle of adapting or improving on nature for the benefit of humans and other species is integral to the lay Jain approach to the environment. For while the ascetic turns his back on nature, withdrawing as far as possible from its demands, lay men and women seek to engage with the natural world in positive ways. Where they adapt and change, they still work with the grain of nature rather than aiming to 'conquer' it. The pharmaceutical company in question maintains itself at a sustainable size and adheres to natural principles as far as it can: whether or not it would accept the label, it is an example of 'Green Pharma' rather than 'Big Pharma'.

Sigma Pharmaceuticals: working with nature's balance

Sigma Pharmaceuticals was founded in 1975 from a community pharmacy in Watford, just north of London, that had been established by the Shah family nine years earlier. Since then, it has become one of the largest distributors of pharmaceutical supplies and products in the United Kingdom, 'employing over 400 people, and servicing over 3000 pharmacies, 1000 hospitals and 600 dispensing doctors throughout the UK and Europe' (Sigma Pharmaceuticals 2014). Its vision is straightforward:

> The world of pharmacy is continually changing. In order to continue to thrive as a business, we must understand the trends and forces that will shape [us] in the future and move swiftly to prepare for what is to come. In very much the same way, we want to help our customers prepare for tomorrow today with the services we provide.
> (Sigma Pharmaceuticals 2014)

This clear and unadorned description of the business is reinforced by the company's mission statement: 'to continually grow (*sic*) a business where we have satisfied customers, satisfied suppliers and satisfied employees' (Sigma Pharmaceuticals 2014). Bharat Shah, Sigma's founder and Managing Director, admits that setting up a pharmaceutical firm involved a process of 'compromise' because 'some products inevitably have animal sources and it is impossible to avoid completely anything that has been tested on animals' (B. Shah 2016). Coming from a strict Digambar background, Bharat knows that some of the most devout Jains would raise objections to this practice, but he believes that members of his community should engage with the world in a practical way, taking 'what is there' and improving on it gradually by making a lasting commercial contribution. Therefore the company adopts a careful strategy, monitoring its stock at regular intervals and appraising its activities so that harm is reduced to a minimum: the principle of alparambhi in action. Bharat also views the pharmaceutical business, when operating within certain parameters, as 'ethical' because of its medical and curative dimensions. Those parameters include respect for the client, concern for the environment and a preference for products produced in conformity with Jain (and other animal welfare) ethics. Bharat regards modern Jainism as a practical philosophy of self-help and community work in which 'the original ideals are more important than the rituals'. He expresses concern that some (but by no means all) younger Diaspora Jains who are rediscovering their heritage 'put the rituals before everything else' (B. Shah 2016).

Sigma has succeeded in its field by maintaining its independence and 'staying within our means'. As Bharat explains, 'we have not got into debt and we do not want to go beyond our capacity'. Thus although the company's mission is to 'grow' and it has successfully fulfilled that objective, the growth takes place within limits and stages, with cooling-off periods of deliberation and stock-taking: 'We have an Annual Meeting once a year of the whole family where we determine our future direction and talk through any problems we face and any changes we need or want to make' (B. Shah 2016). The firm is not 'cashing in' on its success, for Bharat and his fellow directors believe that their profits should be reinvested in the company to improve conditions for staff and efficiency for clients. All the directors are from the same family, who made the transition from the Kenyan textile industry in the 1960s and 1970s; one branch of the family remains in Kenya. The family arrive at decisions by consensus. 'I do not need to talk about leadership according to the standard business model,' says Bharat. 'I express my views and advise and warn. Sometimes we try new things that I haven't expected and if they work we look at them again' (B. Shah 2016).

In one sense, familial control circumscribes the business by excluding external influences. At the same time, it brings its own form of diversification as members of the family (younger members in particular) contribute their own areas of interest or expertise. Expansion into dental and veterinary products, for instance, took place because 'new members of the family came on board' (B. Shah 2016). Aparigraha is also important to the family, which collectively decides what charities to support. The emphasis has been on education, health and disaster relief, with a particular bias towards Africa and India. A good example is the Bangalore-based SHARAN (Sanctuary for Health and Reconnection to Animals and Nature), which promotes healthy forms of eating and naturopathic treatments for diabetes (now epidemic in India's emerging urban middle class) that avoid medicines tested on animals. Support for a charity like SHARAN is, from the karmic perspective, a way of cancelling out or minimising harm, as well as contributing to humane forms of research and therapy and divesting surplus funds as part of Aparigraha.

However, according to Bharat, 'the next generation increasingly wants to see an emphasis on local charities which benefit the communities in which they live, work and intend to remain' (B. Shah 2016). This shift of emphasis reflects a company, and a family, that has embedded itself in the British economy and civil society. Its practice of Aparigraha, and its emphasis on a personal rather than (in Bharat's words) a 'corporate and bureaucratic' service to its clients (many of them independent pharmacies like the Shahs' original business) depends on the family retaining control and avoiding expansion beyond a point where this control is sustainable.

Sigma is a relatively large company with a national base and a network of international connections, although it retains most of the characteristics of a traditional SME. As with so much of commercial practice within Jain communities, it is essential to delve beneath the surface if we are to find the distinguishing features, because they are not loudly proclaimed. While at a superficial level Sigma appears to fit the conventional business model, there are two critical differences from the 'textbook' commercial paradigm. The first of these is a consciousness of natural limits to the size of the enterprise if it is to retain its integrity. The second is that the business should not see itself as an independent actor but as enjoying an interdependent relationship with clients, customers and even rival concerns.

We are back to the central Jain idea of 'binding together'. Applied to business, this translates into what can best be described as an organic theory of commercial development, by which the structure and practices of the company are aligned with human and environmental wellbeing. Such considerations are part of the foundation of the business and have strong cultural roots. In the Jain frame of reference, there is ultimately no separation between the environment and commercial activity.

Bibliography

Shah, B. (2016) Personal interview, 8 April 2016.

Sigma Pharmaceuticals PLC (2014) 'About Sigma Pharmaceuticals PLC'. Available at: www.sigmaplc.co.uk/aboutsigma.aspx. Accessed 10 November 2017.

6　Concluding thoughts

> Society is ... a partnership not between those who are living, but also between those who are dead, and those who have yet to be born.
>
> Edmund Burke, Anglo-Irish politician and philosopher (1790), in Burke (1968: p. 194)

The Jain conception of 'society' matches the vision succinctly expressed above by Edmund Burke. Indeed it surpasses that vision because it also encompasses all forms of life, so that the interest of humanity is seen as one among many interests and hence needs to be balanced against rival viewpoints. Failure to take account of alternative viewpoints from other areas of the natural world, such as animals and plants, can threaten the resilience of human communities. The alienation of humanity from the rest of nature can inhibit constructive economic activities, thus perpetuating deprivation and inequality. For impoverished communities such as those of Bihar, where Veerayatan operates (see Chapter 2), economic independence involves developing a more balanced relationship with nature and acquiring the resources (educational and material) to work with it rather than living in fear. At the other end of the scale, the sponsorship of educational foundations and animal sanctuaries by global financial concerns such as the Jain-owned Meghraj Group or long-established local businesses such as Vardhaman Gems of Jaipur is a way of reminding the owners of these companies of their wider social obligations. Equally, they are reminded of the continuity between human and environmental wellbeing.

This perception of nature is strikingly pragmatic for a faith that is noted for strong or even extreme adherence to the principle that all life is sacred and that interference with natural processes causes harm. For external observers, the behaviour of the ascetics is the most visible manifestation of the Jain belief system, but it is also in some respects the most misleading if we are to make a fair assessment of the Jain approach to nature. Ascetics live out the vow of Ahimsa in as literal a form as possible. Hence their approach differs markedly from the decisions made by lay men and women. They agree to live by the same principle of non-injury, but do so in ways compatible with commercial or professional activities, voluntary work and the life of the extended family and the community. From the Jain perspective, humankind is embedded in nature and so must 'work with' the natural world as far as possible. In this way, the pursuit of sustainable economics and a sustainable 'lifestyle' is the starting point for the application of a system of values based on non-violence and pluralism. Jain thought anticipates the practical concerns of Western environmentalists and the parallel developments in environmental philosophy, in particular the emphasis on holism (see Smuts 1926; Bohm 1980).

Unlike many of the proponents of Deep Ecology (Devall 1990; Devall and Sessions 1985; Naess 2010), nature is not held up as the ultimate point of reference or idealised in its supposedly pristine form. Although there is a similar concern for the 'innate value' of all forms of life, irrespective of their relationship with human needs, there is no belief that nature is in any way 'perfect' or that improvements upon exclusively 'natural' solutions should always be regarded with suspicion. Nor is there the sense of a 'fall', a loss of innocence or the forgetting of ancient knowledge caused by human transitions to urban life. Instead, Jains have always stressed the potential benefits of city living and form overwhelmingly urban communities themselves whether in India or the Diaspora. They attach a high value to education, literacy and scientific progress as civilising forces that increase human knowledge, which is part of the quest for enlightenment that is central to Jain practice. Such knowledge enriches our understanding of how living systems interact (Fortey 1998) and so can make the practice of Ahimsa more effective. The secular goal of freedom conferred by scientific understanding converges with the spiritual goal of freedom from Avidya, or lack of perception (Mardia 2007; Mardia and Rankin 2013). Social development from life in the 'state of nature' (namely dependence on and vulnerability to natural forces) to urban, technologically based communities is seen as part of the evolutionary process and so a part of nature itself.

There is, therefore, no innate division between 'urban' and 'natural', or between scientific reasoning and intuitive wisdom. Reason and intuition are viewed as balancing principles rather than polar opposites. Social (and ecological) imbalances occur when one of these principles is over-emphasised and the other neglected. At the same time, this positive view of scientific and technological progress is accompanied by the strong caveat that knowledge brings power and increases the possibility of inflicting harm. And knowledge, in any case, can only be incomplete, for all but the very few who attain the status of enlightened beings or 'liberated souls'. The doctrine of many-sidedness (Anekant) cautions its devotees to approach the pursuit of knowledge with humility. Far from conferring a sense of infallibility, increased knowledge should make us ever more aware of the limits of our understanding. Thus it expands the range of possibilities, subordinating doctrinaire certainty to a process of continuous qualification. Anekant, and the system of qualified definition known as Syadvada (see Chapter 4), are part of a process of intellectual meditation through which the devotee clears his or her mind of preconceptions, prejudices and absolutist assumptions.

This last aspect of Jain thinking overlaps with the environmentalist questioning of human supremacy, the idea that 'man is the measure of all things' and so has the presumed right to subdue the natural world, subordinating it to human needs or desires. Like environmentalists, Jains see that this 'one-sided' human approach creates distortions both within nature as a whole and in human society. They also connect exploitation of the environment with exploitative relationships between human groups. Jains and environmentalists both regard environmental justice as intimately connected with social justice. Furthermore, many practising Jains might readily identify with the environmentalist demand that humans change or moderate their behaviour and reassess their priorities. The Deep Ecology Platform acknowledges that 'richness and diversity [of life forms] are values in themselves' and that 'humans have no right to reduce this richness and diversity except to satisfy vital needs' (Naess and Sessions 1984). Respect for diversity requires a change in consciousness so that 'appreciating life quality' is favoured over 'adhering to an increasingly higher standard of living' (Naess and Sessions 1984).

In many respects, this position is closely attuned to the Jain principle of Careful Action, whereby encroaching on the rights of other species should take place only when it is 'vital' to do so. Environmentalists emphasise the need to use 'appropriate technology' (Fritsch and Gallimore 2007) that is sensitive to local conditions, including flora and fauna, does not pollute and does not unnecessarily disrupt the natural cycle. Jains are less instinctively suspicious of technology but place greater emphasis on its user's frame of mind, in particular his or her adherence to the Three Jewels of Right Vision (or Viewpoint), Right Knowledge and Right Action. The mental attitude assumes supreme importance because it is the thought that begins the process of activity. An appropriate mental attitude includes the realisation that human progress does not mean separation from the rest of nature, much as personal success does not imply separation from fellow human beings. Both progress and success are transient and subject to sudden reversals.

An important difference between the Jain pursuit of Careful Action and the similar injunctions of environmentalism is that the purpose behind 'care in movement' is ultimately otherworldly, or concerned with transcending the world.

It is here that the ascetic's extreme withdrawal from the commitments and conveniences of mundane existence becomes suddenly relevant to an understanding of Jain philosophy and its workings. Ascetic behaviour reminds Jains of the transcendent nature of the quest for enlightenment. All material actions, however positive, are ultimately karmic and freedom from karma means the cessation of action. The liberated soul or pure life monad rests immobile at the pinnacle of the universe. While acting with care to avoid harm is based at one level on acknowledging connections between all forms of life, at another it represents progress towards non-action and withdrawal from the world. The first, or mundane, level is subordinate to the second, or transcendent, level and the presence of ascetics compels laypeople to remember that Moksha means more than acting with care and performing good works (positive karma). For sympathetic observers, ascetic behaviour is a reminder that although Jainism is in one sense a practical philosophy for life in the world, it is ultimately a faith tradition aimed at personal salvation through transcendence.

All too often, the stance of renunciation adopted by ascetic men and women is taken as a sign of Jain commitment to the environment. In fact, it represents the aspect of Jain Dharma that points the devotee away from the environment towards what is viewed as a more elevated destination. Even the Jain motto, Parasparopagraho Jivanam, is misleading if interpreted as applying wholly to life on Earth. In Jain cosmology, the whole of the vast 'inhabited universe' is teeming with life and so the connections are cosmic as much as earthly. The cycle of birth, death and rebirth is capable of crossing solar systems and galaxies as well as moving between species. Hence Jain philosophy displays a strong bias against assertions of human power over the rest of nature. Such assertions are viewed as ultimately ineffective, in the same way as assertions of 'knowing the truth' are seen as evidence of ignorance.

Jain Dharma is neither a wholly religious nor an exclusively philosophical system. Dharma is the order by which the universe sustains itself, and of which all phenomena within it are part. It is also an ethical system by which human life is aligned as far as possible to the workings of the universe. There is no distinction drawn between theory and practice, between what is thought about or meditated upon and what is lived out. The process of 'self-conquest' to which Jains aspire is an attempt to return to the most authentic or original state of pure consciousness.

Dharma is therefore natural law, but 'nature' in this context differs from what most Western environmentalists understand by the term. Ultimately, it is not the connections between living systems (important though those are), but the point beyond those connections, as yet not fully understood from either scientific or spiritual viewpoints.

When we consider whether the philosophical aspect of Jain Dharma 'qualifies' as environmental philosophy, we come nearest to a satisfactory answer by using the qualified logic of Syadvada: 'it is and it is not'. Viewed from one angle, Jainism is about as far from the concerns of ecological thinkers and campaigners as it is possible to be. It is a search for salvation from the environment and escape from its manifold pressures and constraints. Yet through another facet of the many-sided jewel, it is revealed as one of the most coherent and systematic philosophies of ecological concern devised by humanity. It urges us to tread with care and dignity, to look beneath the surface of things for hidden connections and show respect for all life. Jain communities might be 'self-contained social entities' (Mbiti 1989: p. 253), but their ideas about interconnectedness, cultural diversity and respect for the intelligence of non-human species strike a universal and timely chord.

Bibliography

Bohm, D. (1980) *Wholeness and the Implicate Order*, London: Routledge.

Burke, E. (1968) *Reflections on the Revolution in France*, 1st Penguin edn, London: Penguin Books.

Devall, B. (1990) *Simple in Means, Rich in Ends: Practicing Deep Ecology*, London: Green Print.

Devall, B. and Sessions, G. (1985) *Deep Ecology: Living as if Nature Mattered*, Layton, UT: Gibbs Smith.

Fortey, R. (1998) *Life: An Unauthorised Biography*, 2nd edn, London: Flamingo.

Fritsch, A. and Gallimore, P. (2007) *Healing Appalachia: Sustainable Living Through Appropriate Technology*, Lexington, KY: University Press of Kentucky.

Mardia, K.V. (2007) *The Scientific Foundations of Jainism*, 4th edn, New Delhi: Motilal Banarsidass.

Mardia, K.V. and Rankin, A. (2013) *Living Jainism: An Ethical Science*, Winchester: Mantra Books.

Mbiti, J.S. (1989) *African Religions and Philosophy*, 2nd edn, Oxford: Heinemann.

Naess, A. with Drengson, A. and Devall, B., eds (2010) *The Ecology of Wisdom: Writings by Arne Naess*, Berkeley, CA: Counterpoint.

Naess, A. and Sessions, G. (1984) 'The Deep Ecology Platform', Foundation for Deep Ecology. Available at: www.deepecology.org/platform.htm. Accessed 1 September 2017.

Smuts, J. (1926) *Holism and Evolution*, London: Macmillan and Co.

Glossary

The Jain tradition has a rich vocabulary, drawn both from the classical Sanskrit language and the vernacular Prakrit, known to linguistic scholars as Ardhamagadhi. The list below covers the concepts and expressions used in this study. In the interests of clarity, accents and diacritical marks have not been applied here or in the main text. They are, however, included in the chapter bibliographies where they occur in works cited. In the main text, some Sanskrit or Prakrit words appear with capital letters, others in lower case: this is based both on convention and the original sources in which these terms appear.

Ahimsa   Non-violence, non-injury, avoidance of harm.

Ajiva   Inert matter, insentient object without jiva (life monad or 'soul').

Alparambhi   Requiring minimum violence or harm: used mainly for occupations and trades.

Anekantavada   Principle of 'many-sidedness' (of reality), pluralism or 'multiple viewpoints' (also **Anekant, Anekanta, Anekantvada**).

Anga(s)   Central Jain text(s), (literally 'limbs').

Anu   Infinitesimal or sub-atomic particle.

Anuvrata(s)   Five Lesser Vows undertaken by lay men and women.

Aparigraha   Principle of non-possessiveness.

Asrava   Beginning of 'karmic bondage' (**Bandha**), influx of karmic particles.

Asteya   (sometimes called **Achaurya**) 'Non-stealing', avoidance of theft or taking what is not given.

Astikya   Implicit understanding of the nature of reality.

Avasarpini   Regressive half-cycle of time and the universe.

Avidya   Ignorance, lack of knowledge or perception.

Bandha   Karmic bondage.

Brahmacharya   Celibacy (for ascetics), fidelity and avoidance of promiscuity or exploitative relationships (for lay men and women).

Darshana Perception, (clear) vision.

Dharma Universal law or cosmic order, encompassing philosophy and religion.

Digambar (or **Digambara**) One of the two main schools of Jainism: literally means 'sky-clad' because the most senior male ascetics are naked.

Ekant (or **Ekantika**) One-sidedness, doctrinaire viewpoint.

Eva 'In fact': conveys subjective 'fact' in **Syadvada**, i.e. perceived fact according to speaker.

Gyana (or **Jnana Knowledge**) Knowledge.

Himsa Violence, harm, destructive power.

Irya-Samiti Principle of Careful Action.

Jai Jinendra 'Honour to [the] Jina(s)', 'Hail to the Conqueror(s)', popular Jain greeting.

Jain-ness (Jainness) Cultural sensibility of the Jains.

Jina Spiritual victor, omniscient spiritual teacher (see also Tirthankara).

Jiva Life monad or 'soul'. Sometimes referred to in the plural as **'Jivas'**.

Jiva Daya Sympathy or identification with all sentient beings.

Karma (in Jain thought) Subtle matter composed of karmic particles, attracted to the **jiva** by **Yoga** (activity) and preventing full self-knowledge, omniscience and transcendence of samsara (the cycle of birth, death and rebirth).

Karmon(s) Karmic particle(s): **Karmons** are also referred to as **'Karmas'**.

Kasaya Passion(s), usually negative, such as anger, fanaticism or material greed.

Leshya(s) Karmic colorations.

Lokakasa Inhabited universe, occupied space.

Mahavrata(s) Five Greater Vows undertaken by ascetic men and women.

Maya Deceit, illusion.

Mithyatva (Mithyadarshana) False consciousness, distorted worldview.

Moksha Spiritual liberation, enlightenment, acquisition of omniscience.

Muni Ascetic man or woman.

Naya Viewpoint.

Nirjara Breakage, shedding, falling away of karma/karmic particles.

Nirvana Full enlightenment, moment of attaining enlightenment or becoming a **siddha** or liberated soul.

Panjrapoor Animal hospital or sanctuary.

Papa Negative, destructive or 'heavy' karma.

Parasparopagraho Jivanam Concept of interconnectedness. Philosophical translation: all life is bound together by mutual support and interdependence; religious translation: souls (jiva) render service to one another.

Parigraha   Possessiveness.

Punya   Positive, benevolent, creative or 'light' karma.

Ratnatraya or **Triratna (Tri-ratna)**   Three Jewels of Jainism: **Samyak Darshana** (Right Faith); **Samyak Gyana (or Jnana)** (Right Knowledge) and **Samyak Charitra** (Right Action/Conduct).

Samiti   Rules of conduct for ascetics.

Samsara   Cycle of birth, death and rebirth, process of cyclic change.

Samvara   Stoppage of karmic influx (through awakening consciousness).

Samyak Charitra   Right Conduct.

Samyak Darshana (Samyaktva)   Right Faith.

Samyak Gyana (or Jnana)   Right Knowledge.

Sarvodaya   Principle of 'compassion to all' popularised by Gandhi.

Satya   Truth, truthfulness, honesty.

Shraddha   Educated faith, intuition reinforced by knowledge and reason.

Shuksha   Education.

Siddha   Liberated soul(s).

Sutra   Collection of spiritual aphorisms or teachings, usually in verse form ('thread' or 'string' in Sanskrit).

Svetambar (or Svetambara)   One of the two main schools of Jainism: literally means 'white-clad' because male and female ascetics wear white robes.

Swadeshi   Principle and practice of economic self-sufficiency or self-reliance (popularised by Gandhi and not exclusive to Jains): literally means 'of one's own country'.

Syadvada   System of logic based on qualified definition.

Syat   Expression of possibility in **Syadvada**: literally 'might be'.

Tattva(s)   'Nine Reals', aspects of reality or 'things'.

Tirtha   Ford to be crossed, to which **Samsara** is compared.

Tirthankara   Ford-maker or guide to enlightenment, omniscient spiritual teacher.

Utsarpini   Progressive half-cycle of time and the universe, see Avasarpini.

Vrata(s)   Vow, vows.

Yoga   Activity.

Index

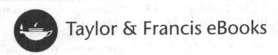